BEN SHEPHARD

humble
heroes

Inspirational stories of hope,
heart and humanity

BLINK
bringing you closer

First published in the UK by Blink Publishing
An imprint of Bonnier Books UK
4th Floor, Victoria House,
Bloomsbury Square,
London, WC1B 4DA

Owned by Bonnier Books
Sveavägen 56, Stockholm, Sweden

facebook.com/blinkpublishing
twitter.com/blinkpublishing

Hardback – 9781788707657
Ebook – 9781788707664
Audio Digital Download – 9781788707671

A CIP catalogue of this book is available from the British Library.

Designed by www.envydesign.co.uk
Printed and bound by Clays Ltd, Elcograf S.p.A

1 3 5 7 9 10 8 6 4 2

Blink Publishing is an imprint of Bonnier Books UK
www.bonnierbooks.co.uk

For all the humble heroes out there: so often hidden,
so rarely celebrated: this is for you.

Contents

Introduction

December 2019, and I am onstage at the Pride of Sport awards. Tonight, we have honoured a fantastic roster of people: alongside the household names of Ben Stokes, Gareth Thomas and Sir Kenny Dalglish, there are others who are stepping into the spotlight for this one night only. So far we've given awards to Mikey Poulli, a ten-year-old who lost his sight at the age of seven but who is still excelling at the football that he loves; and to two community projects that brilliantly demonstrate the power of grassroot sports to bring people together. We've recognised Lord Herman Ouseley, the trailblazing campaigner behind football's Kick It Out campaign. We've met ten-year-old Alfie Fitzsimons, who, after losing his own father to suicide, set up a charity through his beloved football club Everton to support other children going through bereavement. Not to mention the superhuman Josh Llewellyn-Jones, who we'll hear more about later in the book. It's hard to sum up Josh because his sporting feats in support of children with cystic fibrosis simply defy belief, but to see the smiles he puts on the faces of his young troupe of 'CF Warriors' is ridiculously heartwarming.

It's always an emotional night. My job is to keep my feet on the ground and the ceremony swinging along so that each award winner can make the most of their moment, but it would be easy to be swept away. The whole thing always leaves me with a high – the sporting montages, the interviews with friends and family, the footage of thriving community projects – even if I do end up feeling slightly inadequate next to all these superheroes.

We're over halfway through the evening when it's time to meet Corinne Hutton, who is receiving a Special Recognition award. Six years ago, in 2013, Corinne's body was ravaged by the sudden onset of sepsis. Overnight, she went from being a hugely active person, the 'life and soul of everything', a devoted mother who did enormous amounts for charity, to lying in a hospital bed fighting death. 'I was unconscious for three weeks, so I missed most of the fuss,' she said, but six weeks on, though she had survived, her limbs were so badly affected that both hands and both feet had to be amputated. It was then she realised that she had no idea what lay ahead of her. 'How would I be a mum…? Nobody seemed to be able to tell me what life could be like for me.' There seemed to be nowhere she could turn to for answers.

Astonishingly, within weeks of her own life-altering surgery, she set about changing that for others. She set up Finding Your Feet, a charity dedicated to helping amputees find their purpose through sport. Five years on, it has grown from having five members to an organisation that helps more than 3000 amputees at 60 different clubs – Pilates, swimming, climbing, go-karting – whatever helps people get fit, get active and get out there. It has raised over £1.2m, and every year Corinne sets herself a charity challenge, becoming the first double amputee to climb Ben Nevis and Kilimanjaro. At the beginning of 2019 she successfully underwent a double hand transplant. There just seems to be no limit to what she can do.

As the VT chronicling all this rolls to a finish, the audience applauds and Corinne climbs the stairs to the stage, looking fabulous in a red dress. As she reaches me, she gives me a hug and semi-whispers something. At first I don't catch it, and then I realise what it is she has said: 'I feel like a fraud.' This floors me. Here is a woman who has faced an unimaginable setback and channelled it into something so positive for so many people, and *she* feels like a fraud! I reassure her – I hope – but it makes me think. We are celebrating heroes tonight, but not all heroes feel very heroic to themselves.

Corinne's remark prompts another thought: the people coming up on this stage to receive their awards are really only the summit of a gigantic mountain. My mind flips back a couple of weeks to a much less glamorous scene: the hot stuffy conference room where the other judges and I gather round a huge table to get on with the tricky job of deciding who is going to get the nod in each category. By the time it gets to us there is already a shortlist – between five and eight nominees for each award – and we have the slightly absurd job of trying to decide which one is most deserving. To be completely honest, it's an impossible task, but we take it very seriously. We are given the stories behind each nomination, shown videos of what they have achieved and what has brought them there, and then we open it up and discuss who should win. Because of the sportsmen on the panel – they like to win! – these discussions can get quite heated, and there can be pretty vociferous confrontations. You try arguing your case against an impassioned Freddie Flintoff. We all have our favourites, but we know at heart that all of these nominees are something special. Every one of them deserves recognition. We make our cases, we wrangle, we vote, and that leads us to this stage and the well-deserved applause.

But what is really inspiring for me is not just the winners, amazing as they are. It is the knowledge of what they represent. Because for each winner there are five or six others on the shortlist, and for each person on that list there are many more who are nominated. And in turn, for each one of those nominees there are huge swathes of others out there who are quietly getting on with doing things – sometimes extraordinary things, sometimes very simple – that make a real difference to other people's lives. Not for any advancement of their career, not for their own ego or the hope of improving their own standing. They are doing it because for them it is the natural thing to do. These awards – and their big sister awards, the Pride of Britain – are a great way to recognise some of that positive spirit, but they represent a minuscule fraction of the full picture.

I think of it as an enormous net of light and courage and effort and goodwill spreading across the country. In every village, town, borough or parish there are people whose efforts bring a spark of positivity into the world. This isn't just about charity efforts or fundraising: it's about doing things that make life better for everyone. It's about young people from tough beginnings who give their time to mentor those coming up after them. About families who have opened up their homes to refugees in need. About people who organise community litter-picking days or river clean-ups to keep their neighbourhoods beautiful for everyone. They may not all get a shiny award for their mantelpiece, or the recognition of newspaper headlines, but from the ground level up, they are changing the world.

These are the heroes, whether they know it or not. They inspire me every day.

★

I work in an industry – the media – that operates on the premise that fear sells and hope doesn't, and I have always battled with that. It's no secret that social media has made this tendency worse. We consume outrage and fury and anger so easily, and we forget how much courage and positivity and brilliant effort there is out there. My job means I absolutely understand how the news agenda is set and why. I live in a headlines world. But I am lucky that my job also brings me into contact with people who show me that in real life, acts of kindness and hope are in the ascendant.

Every day on *Good Morning Britain* I get a glimpse into the lives of people who represent this side of the coin, something I was reminded of recently when I met Rizwan, a railway worker on the MTR Elizabeth line. He came into the studios during Mental Health Awareness week to tell us how he came to save 29 lives. Two days after doing a Samaritans course in suicide prevention, he was working a cold nightshift when he noticed a passenger on the platform who set off the kind of warning bells he had been told to look out for: dressed in thin clothing and seeming uneasy. Rizwan approached him and, drawing on the techniques he had been taught, simply engaged him in conversation on a neutral subject. They sat down to talk together, and by allowing the conversation to develop, Rizwan let him open up to the point where he revealed he had been intent on taking his own life. That crucial, timely intervention by Rizwan had been enough to make him stand back, and allow the space to get the support he needed.

Since then, Rizwan has gone on to save a further 28 people in a similar way. There's nothing flashy about Rizwan: he speaks softly and carefully, and comes across almost as diffident. But there is a deep-seated humanity there. Doing the Samaritans course has unlocked something in him. It has given him the confidence to draw on the very human skills he already possessed – noticing, listening, caring – to make that crucial difference to people at their very lowest point. It is remarkable what the opportunity to embrace learning and positivity can bring. As he says himself, it sometimes only takes a smile or a friendly word to change someone's day.

Talking to Rizwan crystallised an idea that had been swirling around my brain for a while: that small positive actions can have far-reaching results, and that the more we seek them out and celebrate them, the more power they have. A tiny act can have a huge impact. Rizwan went on that course purely because his employers made it available and he thought he might learn something. It led to 29 life-saving moments. Consuming a constant diet of negative news stories is an easy trap to fall into, but it tends to lead to more anger and more fury and more dread. Luckily, stories like Rizwan's show us that the opposite is also true: the more we engage with hope, the more hopeful we find ourselves, and the more likely we are to put good things out into the world ourselves.

It can feel like on one side of our lives we are bombarded constantly by negative, soul-draining stories, problems that feel too big and intractable for us to face. Meanwhile our cultural narrative, our fiction, is dominated by muscled superheroes – Lycra-clad Avengers and X-Men, great fun for sure, but ultimately caricatures of what strength and courage can be. But on the ground, in our actual lives, most of us know people who are quietly getting on with doing things that make a difference. People who volunteer for children's clubs and sports, spending their weekends for years on end instilling teamwork and loyalty and respect and support into generations of children. Activists who see injustice or inequality and resolve to do something about it. Trailblazers who face their own challenges and strive to make things better for the people who come after them. People who knit the fabric of society together from the ground up through constant effort, care and love.

The coronavirus pandemic meant we all saw the value of local heroes during the worst of the lockdowns: neighbourhood WhatsApp groups being formed to help out shielding neighbours; local businesses doing what they could through their most difficult hours to keep community spirit going; big moments and small that gave us that sense of connection we needed so badly. Famously, we saw everything from the miraculous fundraising efforts of Captain Tom Moore to those small neighbourhood gestures that took on so much meaning. The image that springs to my mind when I think about that first lockdown are the Covid snakes that sprang up all over the country in summer 2020. It was a simple idea: a snake made of painted stones set down on an ordinary pavement, with the intention that people should add their own stone to the end, painted to represent whatever mattered to them. The snakes started small, and then they grew, each stone individually crafted by small hands. It was a reaching out, from each bubble of isolation to all the others, an opportunity for children to connect.

We saw so much of this kind of thing during lockdown: community libraries springing up in people's gardens, online choirs, rainbows in every front window and people knitting tea cosies for postboxes. The mystery benefactor in Warwickshire who brightened lockdown for an entire village by posting charms and keyrings through doors with a cheering poem. Ordinary people who made up large batches of soup and teamed up with local bus services to deliver them to people in need. These may feel like small weapons to wield in the face of a worldwide health crisis, but those moments of connection were vital. They reminded us that, isolated or not, we are all part of a greater whole.

You can spot heroes everywhere, once you start to look for them. Do we celebrate these people enough? Of course, they will sometimes pop up in the 'And finally...' segments of the news. Local newspapers might cover fundraising efforts or community projects, and there will be small 'feel-good' articles in the national press. The Pride awards, which I am honoured to be part of, do a fantastic job of bringing them into the limelight. But there are so many more heroes out there.

The paradox is that many of the individuals I want to celebrate aren't that interested in having the light shine on them, so we have to search them out. But I believe that if we do, that light will reflect back on us in brilliant ways. That is why I wanted to hear more about these everyday superstars. I wanted to find out who is out there in our communities doing amazing things. I started to actively look for these humble heroes, crystallising their experiences first into a series on my Instagram page. It was such a wonderful feeling when I put a call out on social media for nominations, and story after story came winging back to me. In the end I became so addicted to finding heroes that it was clear that they needed another platform, which is how this book came about.

I think of this whole project as a quest – to discover the people out there who, with big acts and small, are changing the world. Because I truly believe that finding them, and celebrating them, will make all our lives shine a little brighter.

★

Why am I so drawn to stories of everyday heroism? I don't know the answer to that, but I do vividly remember my first proper encounter with someone I would class as a hero.

When I was eight or nine I wanted to be an actor, and I was lucky enough to be given my first real acting role. It was in a play at the Edinburgh Fringe, called *Race to be Seen*, about a blind athlete called Graham Salmon. Graham was an extraordinary man: cancer as a baby had led to the removal of both of his eyes, but this didn't hold him back. In the early 1980s, well before Paralympians were lauded in the way they are today, he set the world record for the 100m at the Paralympic Games, and also competed in the 400m and the high jump. But it didn't stop there. Once his career as a runner came to an end he moved on to golf, becoming the only person to hit a hole in one at the Blind Golf Open Championships. There is a wonderful photograph of Graham exploding out of the starting blocks, determination written all over his face, that really sums up his character for me.

Taking part in the play wasn't just a question of being handed a script and being told to learn your lines: the author, Mark Wheeller, worked with Graham through every stage of the script, which meant that Graham came in to workshop the play with us all and was a key part of the journey. He was a huge character, someone who had blazed a trail for people with disabilities and who refused to let anything hold him back.

My role was as 'Young Graham' – Graham as a little boy, finding his place in the world. It was a terrific part. I had one particular line that summed up his spirit and attitude – the young Graham is in a shop with his white stick when a middle-aged woman shouts at him for pretending to be blind. 'It's very disrespectful and rude,' she says.

'I'm not rude,' says Graham. 'I am blind, it's my stick.'

'Don't be so cheeky,' she says. 'How dare you answer me back? I'll be telling your mum and dad!'

There is some back and forth between them before she storms off. I turn, in character, to the audience. A beat. Then: 'Stupid cow!'

Every night, that line brought the house down. The audience loved it, and I loved it even more: imagine being able to say that to a grown-up! Imagine being that brave! For me, that's what Graham was all about. Bravery, and a refusal to be pigeonholed by other people's attitudes.

I adored being in that show. At the time, it was all about the thrill and adrenaline rush of being onstage; that, and the special customised red trainers Graham's sponsor gave me. They were my absolute pride and joy. I just lived in them and I was gutted when I finally couldn't fit into them anymore. But now, in 2022, looking back, I think that one of the best gifts that that experience actually gave me was the chance to meet someone like Graham, someone who had lived his life fearlessly, and in doing so had helped carve the path that later Paralympians would follow. There's a fantastic picture of us together, both rocking dark glasses, in which I am resting my hand on his shoulder, clearly doing all I can to imitate everything about him. How lucky was I at such a young age to get to know him?

I'd love to say this early experience immediately changed me and I became a better, wiser child. Of course in truth I went back to my school and my friends and my rugby and got on with nine-year-old things. But getting to know Graham and what he had gone through definitely stuck with me.

Now, as an adult, I'm in the position where I am lucky enough to take on a lot of challenges to fundraise for charities. It's something I always had a yen to do – I remember wanting to run the London Marathon from when I was 18. Little did I know that not only would I achieve that goal more than once, but that my old friend Ivan Hollingsworth – who we will meet properly later in the book – would rope me into ever more extreme marathon challenges, culminating in seven back-to-back marathons in support of the children's heart charity he has set up.

When I was young, my motivation for challenging myself was simply my desire to push myself physically, test how far I could go and what I would be willing to put myself through to achieve a goal. Once I started working in TV, I was approached by various charities to do more and more, which meant that I could challenge myself and raise money and awareness for great causes at the same time. My job has given me the opportunity to take on some really exciting adventures – climbing Kilimanjaro for Comic Relief, boxing with Lemar for Sport Relief, doing the Palace to Palace bike ride for The Prince's Trust. So what started as a personal challenge had a wider focus. And, of course, the reality is that if you are running for a cause or a charity, or a particular person, you can't stop if it all gets too much!

But perhaps the best thing about the challenges is the kind of people you get to do them with. One image that springs to mind when I think of these challenges is the fantastic Tough Mudder for Tough Mums event that *Good Morning Britain* promoted a few years ago. Tough it certainly was – but so exhilarating also. In the company of some amazing women, my GMB colleagues and I ran through ditches, jumped into freezing water, swam under and over obstacles, and got ourselves thoroughly, thoroughly filthy and exhausted. I remember looking round, halfway through the day, and being surrounded by faces covered in mud and glowing from achievement, and knowing that each of these women had an inspiring story to tell. The whole day was like a physical representation of what the human spirit can achieve, the obstacles it can overcome, and the joy that can result from celebrating that.

I hope this book has that spirit of celebration. It will be about real people, real stories, real heroes. You might not know their faces, and you might not yet know their names – but once you've met them, you'll never forget them.

charity
heroes

Ivan Hollingsworth

Full disclosure: Ivan is one of my oldest friends. This is a man who has dragged me into more pain and agony than you could possibly imagine, but has also given me so many moments of exhilaration, pride and camaraderie that I can't even count them. It feels strange to say that one of your oldest friends is also one of your heroes, but in Ivan's case it is true, because all of it – the pain, the extreme challenges, the laughter – has been in pursuit of an amazing cause and has brought to me and so many others a true sense of purpose. Not to mention the way he has provided joy and healing to hundreds of children who have been through the heart unit at Newcastle's Freeman Hospital.

To go back to the beginning, Ivan and I have pretty much been in each other's lives since before we were born. Our mothers were midwives together, and they were like two peas in a pod: wonderful strong women who would do anything for their loved ones. Both Ivan and I are the youngest in our families, and when I was born Ivan's mum – I called her Auntie Mary because she was like family to me – brought Ivan's sister over to our house and looked after my older siblings so my mum could spend a couple of weeks just concentrating on me. When Ivan was born my mum returned the compliment, looking after all of us older children so Auntie Mary could nurse him. That's how intertwined our families were when we were young. Things changed a little as we got older – Ivan's mum and dad sadly split up and we didn't spend so much time together. But about 20 years ago, Ivan's mum got cancer, and at that point it was as though all the old bonds re-emerged. This terrible ordeal for their family somehow reconnected us all: Ivan's mum and dad, sister and brother, my parents, my brother and sister and me. We'd all gather together round Auntie Mary's hospital bed at the Royal Marsden, and while it was the saddest of times, it was also one of the most emotionally special and hilarious periods of all our lives as well. It is a mark of how amazing she was as a person that even her sickroom was a place where we laughed and told dreadful jokes and talked about things that were real.

Auntie Mary's death was terrible for Ivan. He was only 26 and he had been really close to her. But the way he coped with it is a real mark of his character, as was the fact that he met Nadine, his soulmate, only five weeks after his mum passed away. In his words: 'Some things happen in your life when you're not looking for them, and she was definitely the angel sent to look after me.' I believe – and I know he does too – that he was open to meeting Nadine and falling in love with her at that time precisely because of the legacy his mother had left, and the way that she had handled her final illness. It was almost like a gift his mum gave him – the fact that he wasn't wallowing in self-pity about his loss, the way that his mum had spent her final weeks, meant that he was in a place where he could allow Nadine in. What neither of them knew at the time was that those tools his mum had given him – both in how she lived and how she died – would be tools that he would have to pick up and use a few years later when the two of them faced one of life's hardest struggles together.

Nadine and Ivan got married not long after – a wonderfully happy day – and started looking forward to having a family. It looked at that point as though everything was perfect. Nadine got pregnant, and the pregnancy seemed to be going well: no real red flags, no clinical problems apart from some minor seeming issues with the placenta, just two people blissfully looking forward to the birth of their first baby. Seb was born in 2009 in a midwife-led centre and the birth went ahead smoothly, without clinical intervention. They were both on cloud nine just as you would expect – that mixture of elation, anxiety and pure love that a new baby brings. He was born at night time, at about 10pm, and Ivan was sent home a little while later, expecting to go back in the following morning.

It was about 5am when the hospital called. It was the kind of call no new parent ever wants to receive. They had done some checks and found an anomaly in Seb's heart. Could he come in immediately? Suddenly, instead of bringing their newborn home, 12 hours after Seb's birth Ivan and Nadine found themselves following the blue lights of an ambulance to the heart unit at the Freeman Hospital in Newcastle. When Ivan describes that ordeal, even now, the emotion rises so quickly to the surface: 'You're suddenly being told, 15 hours after your son's been born, that he's got a congenital heart defect. I knew from my previous history that when a consultant and a registrar and a nurse all walk into your room together, they're not telling you that nothing's wrong.' As he puts it, one of them is there to tell you the news, one is coaching him on how to tell you, and the other one is there to pick up the pieces at the end of it.

That third person was definitely needed. It turned out that Seb had a condition called Tetralogy of Fallot, essentially 'four abnormalities with the heart'. The doctors told him the thing that they always say in these circumstances, which is 'Don't google it!' ('Of course, you always google it,' says Ivan.) They followed this up by saying, 'Go home, we'll speak to you in the next few days, but he's going to need heart surgery within the next one to two years.' And so, shellshocked, Ivan and Nadine took Seb home.

It's a quick thing to say – surgery in the next couple of years – but just for a minute imagine how that felt. They were looking at their tiny baby – Seb was born at only 5lb – knowing that there was something badly wrong with the very organ that should be keeping him alive. Worse still, they knew that to fix it a doctor was going to have to cut his chest open and perform major surgery. Taking a newborn home from hospital is terrifying for any new parent; exceptional and joyous as that moment is, the responsibility of having to care for this tiny scrap who depends on you for everything is overwhelming. But the extra layer of fear that they had to deal with is just incomprehensible. To compound the agony, Ivan's best friend had died of undiagnosed cardiomyopathy when he was only

27, and Nadine's brother had died of the same thing at the same age. There was a huge level of associated grief, and a deep-rooted fear throughout the whole family.

The hardest thing was that the hospital had told them that one feature of the condition was that Seb might periodically have something called a 'blue spell', when part of the heart muscle would go into spasm, causing deoxygenated blood to be pumped the wrong way round the body. They would know this was happening, said the doctors, because Seb would cry 'a different sort of cry', and as soon as that happened they should lay him on his back, gently press his knees to his chest to release the spasm and call the hospital immediately.

Well, thought Ivan, I've only had him for a couple of days, with the greatest respect I'm not sure how much help 'a different sort of cry' is to me. You can imagine how quickly Ivan and Nadine rushed to their son's side every time they heard him give even the slightest wail. In the end, Seb was five weeks old when he first had one of these spells, and that's when they found out what 'a different kind of cry' meant: the noise was like that of a wild animal in pain, while his skin took on an ominous bluish grey colour.

Because Seb had been so small at birth the doctors wanted to wait until he was a year old before the surgery, hoping he would grow enough to balance out the risk and reward of such a serious procedure. But at about 14 weeks he had a massive spell, one that lasted about half an hour. It was clear that he couldn't wait any longer. The clinical team was alerted, and Seb was moved to the top of the surgery list.

When I think about that operation and what it involved, it just astounds me, and I know it astounds Ivan. The surgical team had to crack open Seb's chest, stop his tiny heart and lungs, and put him on a bypass machine. Only then could they start to repair the heart. Now, as Ivan puts it, your heart is about the size of your fist, so just picture how tiny this little baby's heart was. He was still only 16 weeks old.

Only one parent was allowed to go and be with Seb as they put him under the anaesthetic. It was Nadine that went, and Ivan had to kiss him goodbye in a corridor and watch him be wheeled into surgery. What Ivan went through as he watched his son and wife, his whole family, disappear through the doors, is heartbreaking: 'Nadine went off with him and I just sat there. I was just sobbing my eyes out because I knew that might be the last time I would see him alive... My whole sense of my job as a parent, my job as a dad, was to look after, to protect, to keep safe, and I just had no control here.'

The operation was six and a half hours long. The surgeon, Dr Hassan, had to patch up the heart, cut away some of the muscle and, astoundingly, cut the pulmonary artery lengthways – because it is so narrow – so that he could open it out to mend it. Nowadays, Dr Hassan is a friend of Ivan's, and he admits that he sometimes catches himself looking at the surgeon's hands and realising that they once were right inside his infant son's chest, performing the most delicate of operations to make him whole.

At last, the surgical team finished and were able to return Seb to his parents. But even when the six-hour ordeal was over, and had gone well, he still had to have intensive care. On the wall of Ivan's study still hangs a photo of the tiny Seb, wires and tubes attached, lying in his cot in the intensive care ward. It's a picture that makes you catch your breath: the devices keeping him alive look so alien, so invasive on that little body. Ivan took the photo on the night that Seb's condition suddenly worsened. He genuinely didn't know if it was the last time he would see his son, and knew that this shocking image might be the last photo he would ever take of him.

But Seb rallied. From that point he started to improve, and Nadine and Ivan found themselves 'getting nearer to the door', as Ivan puts it, first of all being moved to the general ward and, finally, about five or six weeks after the surgery, being allowed to go home.

It was as though the starting clock for their family had been reset. Seb's heart had been patched and was now working. They could expect that he would not have any more blue spells. But Seb was still under the care of the heart unit: he would need constant monitoring as he grew to see that his heart could cope, and they knew that a further surgery still lay in his future. Ivan and Nadine were left to process the trauma they had been through and work out how to be the husband, wife, and parents they wanted to be. There was relief, but also a huge cascade of shock and grief about what had happened, a grief that seemed all the more difficult to understand and process because Seb had pulled through.

★

All of this was a huge ordeal, and I was in awe at the time of the courage and grace with which Ivan and Nadine got through it. But why does it make Ivan a hero? That is a story that started one night in intensive care, in the days after Seb's operation. To rewind a bit, Ivan has always been a keen runner, competing in middle-distance events at a regional level. It happened that a couple of weeks before Seb's surgery, he and I and another friend had taken part in the smallest marathon in the world – the Tresco marathon in the Isles of Scilly. This was a wonderful race that ran annually for nine years, inspired by one of the local hoteliers there who had always wanted to run the London Marathon and couldn't because it comes at the beginning of the tourist season. Because of this, the landowner there – Tresco is an interesting place, an island owned by one individual – decided to hold a marathon on the island instead. It would comprise seven and a half laps of the entire island, through some absolutely beautiful scenery, and because the hotelier who inspired it has a son with cystic fibrosis, the money raised would go the CF Trust, which is a charity I am involved with.

When they asked me, well before Seb was born, if I wanted to participate, I said yes straight away, and asked if I could bring along Ivan and Andy, a friend of Ivan's through running circles. By the time the race came around, Seb had been born and, in the condition he was in, Ivan assumed he shouldn't go, but Nadine made him a deal. Yes, he could go, but on one condition: that he win it.

This was a bit of a tall order: one of the other competitors, who had won every year since the competition started, was a renowned international champion. *Yeah, right,* I thought to myself when Ivan told me on the start line that he had to win. But I shouldn't have been surprised when he crossed the finish line in first place: Ivan is one of the most determined people I know.

All of this made a nice story for the local newspaper back at home, and the clipping was pinned above Seb's bed in intensive care. On the very day that Seb began to pick up, and the nurses came to remove his wires and tubes, Ivan and Nadine turned to each other and knew that they had to do something, anything, to say thank you to the hospital and the people there who had done such an amazing job. 'I didn't know how you thank people who save your son's life,' says Ivan, 'but I knew we were going to have a damn good go.' His gaze fell first of all on the machine – all flashing lights and beeping sounds – that had been their constant companion, monitoring Seb's condition day and night (and traumatising his parents when it beeped, flashed or whirred in alarm).

'How much is one of those?' he asked.

'About £120,000,' came the answer.

'Right, well we'll buy you one,' said Ivan. Of course at that point he didn't have a clue how he was going to do such a thing: 'We're not rich and we're not famous,' he added, 'so it may take a while, but we will get there.' Clearly, this was going to involve more than taking part in the odd fun run or baking some cakes.

The second part of Ivan's inspiration came when he caught sight of the clipping of him crossing the finish line in Tresco. Running had been something that he had always done, and he had reached a pretty good level. 'But,' he says, 'as a skill in life it probably doesn't do much for you unless you're going to win the Olympics or something.' Nevertheless, at that moment, in that hospital room, looking at his vulnerable child, at the machine that had helped save his life, and at the scrap of newspaper pinned above the bed, an idea began to form.

That idea would grow into Ivan's first Coast 2 Coast challenge. There is an established cycling route that runs from one side of the country to the other, from Whitehaven over to Tynemouth, which is close to where Ivan lives. *Well,* thought Ivan, *I can't cycle that, but I can run.* He and Andy looked at the route, and realised it could be perfectly split into five marathons. Bingo. They could run five marathons on five successive days in aid of the heart unit. Only one problem: Ivan wasn't a distance runner – his event was usually the 1500m, running in circles round a track. The Tresco marathon had been his first and only distance event. Still, how hard could it be?

★

This was the point at which I got roped in, and WhatsApp messages went out to some others, and finally there we were in Whitehaven, five of us, with support vehicles provided by family and friends. The idea was we would complete the five-day challenge on behalf of CHUF, the Children's Heart Unit Fund, host a black-tie and posh-frock dinner, and see how much could be raised. I remember that moment well, laughing and joking around before we set off, teasing each other about how easy it would be... Well, little did we know.

Speaking for myself, those five days would be some of the most extraordinary I have known. From the very start, we had a sense of doing something bigger than ourselves. It's an exhilarating experience, putting yourself through an ordeal like that, knowing that you're all in it together. It wasn't just about the money raised for a great cause, or the fact that we were pushing ourselves to our limit, fantastic though both those things were. It was the sense of shared endeavour, that together we were able to do so much more than we would have managed alone. It wasn't just the other runners either: it was the fantastic backup team too: Ivan and Nadine's old friends, Sarah Jones and the Norgates, not to mention Nadine herself. She was the unsung hero of the whole enterprise, leading the support team, sorting logistics, planning the routes, securing our overnight stays and making sure we were fed and rested so we could go again the next day. She would drive alongside us and distract us from the pain by taking the mick out of us or playing loud music, pick us up if we fell over, guard us from the traffic... and all this while looking after Seb, who was still a tiny boy in the back of the car. It was truly a team effort.

During that time I experienced more highs and lows than I could possibly describe, but it's probably summed up best in the run into Carlisle on the second day. By the afternoon, we'd run about 19 miles, setting a reasonably relaxed pace of about four miles an hour. There wasn't much left in the tank for any of us – we'd already run a whole marathon the day before, but we felt we were just about on track. That was until I got a call from the cameraman who GMTV were sending up to do a piece on us.

'Ben,' he said, 'I'm in Carlisle.'

'Great,' I said. 'We're probably about six miles away.'

'Fine,' he replied. 'Well, you've got an hour to get here, because I have to turn the footage round and get it down to London for tomorrow morning.'

I looked at my watch. Right. 'OK, guys,' I said. 'We've got one hour to run six miles.'

We all looked at each other. We were already exhausted, and we knew we'd have to run the fastest we had ever run even to have a chance of making it. But we also knew the value this publicity would bring to the charity. We had two choices

– either just say, 'Well, there's no way, we're not going to get there,' or…

'We've just got to go for it,' said Ivan, 'See if we can make it.'

So we ran. We organised ourselves a bit like a Tour de France peloton: two of us up in front setting the pace, two at the back and one in the middle. The frontrunners would go as fast as they could, and when they tired, they would drop off to the back and the next people would move up, and we did this for the final six miles. It was just an extraordinary feeling. Out of nowhere we found all these reserves of energy, and a single-minded focus that took us over as a group. We all knew that we were in it together. As we were running we just had that unshakeable conviction that we could look to the left or to the right, in front or behind, and know that the person there had our back and was willing us on. Nobody would be left behind. Ivan has a saying: 'When you eliminate the chance you're not going to make it, then you start figuring out how you are going to succeed.' That communal spirit was the rocket fuel we needed.

The moment we finally crossed the line in Carlisle it felt as though we'd just won the Olympics – the most exhilarating feeling, just pure joy to have all got there, all made it. It wasn't because the cameras were there, or because we'd hit a particular goal, it was just knowing that we were doing something together, something that was really worthwhile.

Having said that, there was a moment we were all high-fiving and celebrating, chests pumping and legs weak from the effort. And suddenly we looked at each other and the realisation dawned: we'd be doing the whole thing again tomorrow. And the day after. There's no doubt this C2C that Ivan had dreamed up was a beast of a challenge. But there was always something to boost us, people joining the route as we ran, or just the sense that we were doing this for other kids like Seb. By the time we were on our final approach into Tynemouth on the last day, we were joined by about 30 people who ran alongside us, and the feeling was simply incredible.

Ivan puts it best: 'I just knew we'd got something here... I didn't care about the money, I didn't care about the profile... It was about connection, about shared goals, about the ordeal you go through together... that lightbulb moment of "I don't know where this is going, but it's going to be bigger than we ever could have anticipated".' And he was right.

★

That first Coast 2 Coast challenge raised £18,000 for CHUF. That was great, but Ivan had no intention of stopping there. The next year, he decided to add to the challenge, so we ended up cycling the route for two days in one direction, and then running back. In all there were seven Coast 2 Coast challenges – over the years he drew other runners in, and there were more and more people wanting to take part and raise money. Ivan was always mindful though that this whole thing was no ordinary run. It was about repaying the heart unit, about a collective commitment to something larger than just the individuals running. When it threatened to get so big that the core vision was being lost, he pulled it back to its basics.

Alongside the Coast 2 Coasts, Ivan also set himself solo challenges: first – and I still can't get my head around this one – he decided to run 100 miles in 24 hours. 'I was trying to work out what I could do that could take the profile to another level,' he says. The 100 miles in 24 hours is seen as one of the ultra-endurance benchmarks. It's a very different mindset to a normal race, however long: knowing you're going to be on your feet for 24 hours, knowing you have to hit that target in that time, dealing with the inevitable sleep deprivation.

Ivan set his route from Eyemouth in the Scottish Borders, finishing once again in Tynemouth. Once again, the indefatigable Andy would run along with him for support and encouragement. Ivan trained hard, got into the best shape he possibly could, and revved up as much publicity as possible. ITV covered his preparation, the date was set, and he was ready to go when he hit a problem with his thigh muscle. Suddenly, he couldn't even run for training sessions, and found himself having to prepare for this epic run by cycling instead. But there was no way he could put the date off without losing all the publicity he had created.

On the day, he got the physio to tape him up, made it to the start line, and within 30 minutes of running – he had just reached the Scottish border – he felt the right quad go into spasm. 'It's quite painful when you have cramping muscles and you've got 23 and a half hours to go,' he says with some understatement. An hour after that, the left one started cramping, too. His lowest point was at the halfway mark. By now they were an hour and a half behind schedule, both his legs were in spasm, it was the middle of the night, and he was absolutely exhausted. To make it worse, it was clear that Andy was really struggling physically. Ivan knew he was going to have to tell his best mate, after 51 miles of running, that he should stop. This might be where you and I would think about giving up, but don't forget Ivan's mantra – once you eliminate the possibility that you're not going to make it, you find ways of making it work. He just wasn't going to allow stopping to become a possibility: 'When we stop the challenge, the pain stops, the fight stops. But for children like Seb, the fight goes on every single day.' Now running solo, Ivan locked down, and set about making up for the time he had lost.

Somehow, he did it, and completed the challenge with half an hour to spare.

There isn't the room to go into all the different ways that Ivan and Nadine have found to raise money for the heart unit. Charity balls, charity training sessions, Great North Runs… On one occasion he even skied 10km downhill dressed in a mankini. I didn't do every C2C challenge with him, but the ones I did tested me to my limits. On one bike ride the gradient was so steep that I had to dismount and push the bike uphill, wearing cleats, the angle so severe that the bike was above my head as I struggled through in the freezing rain. Luckily, in the next one Ivan threw in a swimming element, and I managed to get the better of him there, much to his surprise.

By 2017 the Seb4CHUF charity had raised £480,000. Ivan was determined to find one grand idea to bring the donation total to over the £500,000 mark. The answer to this was the Half the Country, Half a Million challenge: to go halfway up the country, from London's Marble Arch to Newcastle. For this, he would cycle 260 miles, and then get off the bike and run a double marathon, finishing at the doors of the heart unit where the journey had started nine years before.

Ivan trained to within an inch of his life – he was in the best shape he could possibly be, he had a body fat count of less than 4 per cent, he had been training two to three times a day for months. Everything was lined up. But the weather was not on his side. Going across The Fens, the flattest part of the country, the weather picked up until there were crosswinds of over 40mph hitting the bike: 'The plan had been that I would just lock in, I had two support crew cycling with me and I would just sit in the middle and get the benefits. But the wind started smashing from all sides, and the trucks were going past and it was just horrific. It was so dark so all you could see was the flashing light of the bike ahead, and your brain starts to play tricks on you. And then my adductor muscles started to spasm.'

But all his previous physical ordeals had taught him well: 'One thing I've realised over these challenges: the brain's ability to change the calibration of pain is fascinating.' In spite of the pain, he had confidence that he could use the power of his own mind to overcome it. 'I decided to count the revolutions of my left knee. I thought if I focused on my left knee rather than my right leg then I could change my brain.'

Ivan counted to about 13,000 revolutions, and once he had reached that target he started to count the revolutions of the pedal of the bike ahead of him. Once his count had reached 12,000, he found that his leg never spasmed again. It was almost as though the counting had put him in a kind of hypnotic trance. Interestingly this was something he had actually trained for: he knew that in a challenge like this, at some point the pain would become unbearable. Part of his preparation was precisely targeted to his mental state; he would train in the hardest of conditions: 'When it's your thirteenth session of the week and you are physically and mentally spent, and making that the hardest session, that's hard, but it means that when you get into the darkest possible moment, then you're not searching for the tools to deal with it.'

The whole challenge took 32 and a half hours, stopping only for a ten-minute power nap when he found himself falling asleep on the bike. Eventually, he made it: Ivan's fundraising journey ended where it had begun: at the doors of the heart unit where the tiny Seb had been rushed all those years before. Waiting to greet him on the steps was Seb himself, now a happy nine-year-old boy, Seb's little sister Immy, who was born seven years after Seb, and of course Nadine. Not to mention a phalanx of press reporters, all helping to raise money and raise awareness. Ivan had reached his target, raising over £500,000 in total. He had put his body through hell to achieve it, but he knew that those 24 hours of physical torture were as nothing to the parents who were sitting in the intensive care ward, or for the patients themselves. Whatever Ivan has put himself through, it's a fraction of what those children have endured at such a young age.

As to what all that money was used for, that is what makes my heart soar: 'The first year or so the money we raised bought some kit because that's what they needed,' says Ivan. But as the sums of money raised grew and grew, he and Nadine realised they could do something more ambitious. The equipment they had bought was important, of course – some of it was literally lifesaving – but Ivan began to think bigger. He reflected on what the whole spirit of his challenges had been. 'We weren't professional athletes, we were just a bunch of absolute clowns coming together, and the fun we had, and the element of joy that came through, and the positivity – we needed to do something that fitted with that but also had purpose.' He wanted the money to result in something that reflected that spirit.

Ivan spoke to the staff on the ward – Lesley Hamilton, the Nurse and Ward Manager, and Joanne Moore, the nurse who led the play team, who immediately said, 'What about a playroom?' There was already one attached to the heart unit, but it was small and old, with nothing in it to inspire. Thinking back to his time there with Seb, and realising that some children would spend months if not years on the ward, Ivan saw that a proper place for them to play in could be transformative. The design of the hospital already allowed for a dedicated playroom for the unit, one which would have space both indoors and outdoors, but as yet there was nothing to fill it. Ivan saw his chance to do something amazing with the money he had raised. He was allowed to be involved in discussions with the architect right from the beginning, and his brief for the project was pretty simple: 'We need to make this the best damn playroom in the country,' he said.

And they more than fulfilled that ambition. I remember visiting the space when it was still in construction – all concrete walls and plaster dust – but nothing could prepare me for the Willy Wonka-style children's play factory it has turned out to be. Just to walk into the room lifts the spirits: coming from the heart ward into the playroom is like going through the looking glass, or through the wardrobe into Narnia. It's an oasis of joy and colour and fun, a wonderful space, flooded with daylight, with big doors and windows that lead out on to the garden. Outside, there is a fantastic track for the children to race their pedal cars around. Inside, there are toys and games everywhere, beanbags, bookshelves, computer consoles, drawing materials, everything a child could possibly want. In every corner there are families sitting reading books or playing games, or just being together.

For me, the spirit of the place is summed up in a magical moment I witnessed on one of my visits: a pair of small children, clearly brother and sister, raced through the room to get outside. It was clear that the boy was very unwell and was wheeling with him a piece of medical equipment. But as he jumped into a pedal car, folded the medical device in with him, and his sister began to push him, the differences between him and his sister melted away. In that space, the illness was incidental: they were both just lost in the magic of play. That was what Ivan and the team sought to create: somewhere where the medical side of these children's lives is catered for but which doesn't govern their being. A space where they can be safe and looked after and monitored if necessary (there are plugs both inside and outside for them to plug in equipment if they need to), but where they can also just be children, children who create and explore and flourish. That is what the playroom has done. As Ivan says, 'If you can create an environment where kids feel like they can play, then that's part of healing.'

It is wonderful to visit the playroom and know that my aching legs and knackered joints played a very tiny part in bringing it to life. But mostly I feel huge pride in Ivan, knowing that this place was conjured up by his inexhaustible energy, determination and imagination. It was always really important to Ivan that it was Seb's name above the door of the room. Throughout all his challenges he was determined that everyone who participated or gave money should understand that one thing lay behind all of the fundraising efforts: hope. Hope is what Seb represented: a tiny infant who faced and overcame huge challenges from day one.

These days Seb is a fantastic 13-year-old boy – a terrific artist and illustrator with an inexhaustible knowledge of the Marvel universe, and a real talent for Taekwondo. He has definitely inherited his father's focus and determination. It has not been entirely plain sailing. Ivan and Nadine know he will be facing surgery again soon, and probably periodically for the rest of his life. Throughout his childhood they have had to tread the balance between the instinct to protect him and allowing him to push himself, flourish and grow. I know they've done a fantastic job of it.

★

I started this piece about Ivan by talking about his mum and the legacy she left him. And I want to finish with her too, because I think what is most heroic about Ivan is not his physical feats, or the pain he has put himself through, or the money he has raised. It's his attitude, the attitude she fostered in him, one where you do what you can to give back to others. In his words: 'It's that thing of being in service. She taught me that a life of service and a life for others makes your life richer as a result.'

When Ivan looked around that intensive care ward during one of the darkest times in his life and vowed to help them in any way he could, that attitude came shining through. That's what life is all about, for him: finding opportunities, big and small, to make other people's lives a little bit brighter. There's no doubt that Ivan has done this: for the children on the heart unit of course, for his family, and for all of us who have participated in his challenges. In doing so, he would say, he has made his own life that much richer. It's not about the extraordinary scale of the challenges, or the sums of money involved. It's about the spirit with which he does it, one that isn't about ego, but brings everyone else along with him.

As he puts it: 'You remember how it made you feel, you remember the run into Carlisle and the fact that four other guys had your back. That is the legacy of what we did... Yes, we raised money for the heart unit, but it was the way that what we did made people feel special. Anybody can do that.'

Not many of us could run, cycle or swim as far as Ivan has. Not many of us will find ourselves raising half a million quid and creating a wonderful playroom for the children who need it most. But all of us can take on a little bit of his spirit, and look for the places where we can make a difference, too.

Carrie Byrom

Near a village in Lancashire, well-hidden down a track indicated only by a modest wooden sign, is a place where a certain kind of magic happens. This is Parbold Equestrian Centre, not just a riding school but also the base for Stable Lives, a charity where humans and animals come together to heal people whose lives have been shattered by trauma. 'A calm place for a stable life' is the charity's motto, and the green countryside and gentle hills do make for an idyllic setting. There are horses grazing in the fields, looking over the doors of their wooden stables, or being exercised in well-kept arenas, and there's always a dog or two trotting around. The centre is quiet and tucked away – even some people in nearby villages barely know it's there, making it even more of a haven, but it is easily reached by train from Liverpool and Manchester, so it feels accessible as well as private. Everything about the place declares safety, welcome and warmth, because this is somewhere where people can come when life has become too much, and learn that life is not just about survival; it's about joy and camaraderie and self-worth.

All of this is the brainchild of Carrie Byrom, who has been at the riding school since her mother bought it when she was a young girl, and who now manages it. Five years ago, Carrie was already a seriously impressive person. For a start, she was an international Three Day Event rider, with the Olympics in her sights. I'm not that used to horses myself, so this is a sport that absolutely amazes me: men and women who are able to tune themselves into these gigantic animals and harness their strength and elegance to perform athletic feats. I watch them jumping huge solid fences or persuading their horses to do the most delicate manoeuvres in the dressage arena and I can't even imagine what that takes. For Carrie, though, horses are not just part of her sport – they are woven into the fabric of her life and always have been. She has a particular affinity for rescue horses: many of the animals at the centre have been rescued from difficult lives or mistreatment, and so Carrie was also involved in their rehabilitation. And on top of this, she was running Stable Lives, the charity she had developed to use equine therapy to help children who were finding it difficult to cope in mainstream schools or struggling with their behaviour. Back then, in 2017, this was the main focus of the charity, and it was having fantastic results. Word had spread among the schools in her area. So her life was definitely busy, just how she liked it.

All of this was to be seriously challenged when, in April that year, a bad fall on a cross-country course derailed Carrie's eventing career. With one elbow badly broken and the other wrist in smithereens, she knew that she was going to be facing a series of difficult operations, and that her eventing career was at the very least going to have to be put on hold. Carrie has a strong Christian faith, and has always believed that there is a plan for everyone, but it was very hard to understand what that plan was now. Suddenly, everything that had seemed to be in her future disappeared. It isn't in her nature to do nothing – she describes herself as a 'very busy, do-ey person' – and she literally felt broken. In the weeks after the accident, she went to a Christian festival and found herself one night sitting by an empty stage, entirely alone and sobbing. Just then, in a moment of serendipity, she became aware that the screen next to the stage had blinked into life and onto it flashed an advertisement for a group of entrepreneurs who were offering help with charitable enterprises. There was a series of questions, starting with: 'Do you have an idea that might change people's lives?'

Yes, thought Carrie, and by the time the rest of the questions had run through, she realised that she needed to do what she always did when she hit challenges, which was to think: 'OK, that's happened, now how do we spin it around?' and in particular, how could she spin it around in a way that would most help others?

The answer, of course, lay with Stable Lives.

★

It was around this time also that something else ignited in her: she began to realise that the equine therapy that was having such a great effect on children might also help support the recovery of adults who had been through trauma. In particular, coming from a background with military connections, she began to think of how the charity might be able to help military veterans or blue-light emergency service workers like paramedics or firemen who were recovering from PTSD, as well as survivors of domestic violence or victims of crime. Anybody who needed a place to rest, recuperate and reconnect with themselves and the rest of society.

Up to this point, Stable Lives had been 'ticking along', in her words, but she knew that if it was going to grow, money would be needed to provide a proper base for it within the yard. She came up with the idea of a yurt, which would be the perfect headquarters. The only problem was money: there wasn't enough to buy one. Which was why she decided to undertake a 24-hour ride to raise funds: less than two months after the fall that shattered her arms and her dreams, she found herself undertaking the ride of her life, keeping going for a whole day straight on a succession of different horses. 'It was a *stupid* plan,' she says, laughing, now, 'but I did it because I knew I could sit on a horse for 24 hours, I knew I could ride with one hand. I knew I had access to enough horses that we could just rotate them through, and I needed to do something because I had to practise what I preach.'

With the seed money raised from this, she was able to put in the yurt that forms the hub of the Stable Lives organisation. It's a cheerful place, instantly welcoming even from the outside, and bright and warm once you step in. The yurt is the centre of operations; as people arrive the fire inside will be lit, the good biscuits will be out, and the kettle will be on. (Carrie is a great believer in the power of a good cup of tea and a biscuit.)

A typical course is six weekly sessions – in groups for adults, or one-to-one for children. I spoke to Carrie the day before a new adult course was about to start, and you could tell how excited she was to get going: 'I know that everybody's nervous about stepping foot onto the yard, but I also know that by weeks three or four the banter's started, everyone's a team, everyone finds their little nook that they're happy with.'

Above all, from the first moment people arrive at the yard, they are made to feel safe and welcome. Even Carrie's little dog Percy gets on board. Over the years, Carrie has noticed that Percy is unerring in always picking out from a group the very person who needs the most support. Without any prompting, he will always head over and sit beside them. For the same reason, Carrie usually prepares for a child's first one-on-one session by having her other dog Tiger ready and waiting on a lead. If they seem particularly nervous or scared by these new surroundings, she hands Tiger over and asks them to look after him while they walk around. It's enough to break their internal focus and lower those barriers a little.

Carrie is a strong advocate for the power of chat, fun and good banter: in the yurt there is a box called the Titterbox. She encourages people to write down their memories of the day to put in there, something that made them laugh, something that helped them connect: 'Our vision of the course is that everyone goes away with some of those memories they can pull out when they need them.' The first priority is simply to get to know each other – every morning starts with a group discussion. There will be a thought for the morning that invites people to reflect on what has brought them here, but without any requirement to share that with others. Usually, only Carrie is privy to their particular challenges – whether it is trauma brought on by the work they do, or a crisis they have been through, or a specific mental health difficulty. Everyone is given a workbook to guide them through the horsemanship they will learn (the steps of the course are based on the British Horse Society's stable management course, and most people will come away from it with a certificate), and then it is out to the yard to meet the animals.

Later, there will be lunch, which again brings the participants together, for good food and conversation – the chemistry that the groups always form is a source of great joy to Carrie. The afternoons are usually taken up by a practical community project – perhaps building benches for the canal in the village. Carrie has found these invaluable for igniting old passions and stoking new interests. People have gone on from her courses with renewed enthusiasm, and in some cases new directions: one graduate went on to become a photographer, having been reminded what it is that he loved to do.

If you, like me, don't fully understand how horses can help children and adults recover from their difficulties, it is fascinating to hear Carrie explain. Equine therapy, at its heart, uses the principle of using a horse as a method of opening up different ways of talking about hard-hitting topics, without any sense of judgement. Although mental health difficulties are wide-ranging and complex to treat, Carrie believes that recovery can be supported by keeping the basics very simple: 'There are certain things you can do to help – eating right, drinking right, exercise, the right social groups. If you sit down and talk to these children and adults and say you've got the balance of all these wrong, then they instantly start to turn off.' But if you put that individual together with a pony and encourage a bond, then the focus shifts.

It is not just humans that Carrie is helping. Around three quarters of their 31 horses are rescue animals. This is a crucial element of the work: the yard has always been based around rescue animals, partly because Carrie is 'a sucker for a sad story', and partly because there simply wasn't that much money floating around when the family started at the stables. But the fact that the horses themselves have overcome their own difficulties is a huge part of how the programme works. Simply describing what the pony has been through and what challenges it has had to overcome can open the conversation in a completely new way. It's all about using horses as teaching aids – 'taking out the human and putting in an animal,' as Carrie puts it.

What does this look like in practice? Stable Lives works with a lot of military and ex-military people, and, as Carrie explains, 'If I go in and say to them, "Your body language is really aggressive, you slam doors, you shout, that's why you're getting into fights," then that really wouldn't work.' But if she asks the same person to enter an arena, walk over to a pony, put on a headcollar and lead it back, that simple action can be very revealing. 'I know for a fact that if they walk in fast and slam the gate then that pony is going to run away.' So if she then explains to them that they need to lower their shoulders, take a breath, walk slower and approach more gently, not only will the pony come to them this time but there is a whole opportunity to talk about body language. Even just the physical sensation of stroking a horse's soft muzzle or brushing their coat can be calming – 'you can see the heart rates start to come down.'

★

One important aspect of Carrie's role is to pair each person who comes to her with the right horse. So a child who struggles to be calm and relaxed might be paired with a pony that has been rehabilitated and who has some of the same challenges. 'So instead of us sitting down and saying, "You've got to calm down, you've got to relax", we can tell them how the pony has recovered. It's a less intense, softer way of doing it. Many times, the children, or adults, will reflect on the horses and say, for example, "What did Mole do to get through this? What did Bumble do?"'

Mole, for instance, was a horse that she acquired about three years ago. His owner, very sadly, had taken her own life and left behind two horses who were not in a good state because she hadn't been in a place where she could take care of them. Mole was 'just a complete hooligan', who didn't trust anybody, and was quite aggressive in his behaviour. Carrie knew that the reason he was aggressive was because he was frightened. As an experienced rider, she tried everything she could with the horse, but she was in the process herself of recovering from her accident, and found that she was having to force herself to try and ride him. With any rescue horse, she explains, you have to be a bit of a detective: they can't tell you what has happened that hurt them, so you have to progress slowly and take everything as it comes. With Mole, she tried everything, even bringing in a friend who was a film stuntman, and he couldn't do it. Mole refused to have anything to do with him. So Carrie had to dig deep herself: 'I had to reflect on myself and tap into my confidence again, and I think that horse came into my life really to build me up again and make me realise that I did have the skillset to do it and I just had to get on with it.'

Nowadays, she believes, Mole is a world-class eventing horse. For children with challenging behaviour, Mole's story can be transformative: 'They really get it: that sometimes what comes across as bad behaviour is just them scared and anxious and afraid.' Carrie tells them that when Mole used to get anxious or frightened he would try and bite or squash her or fight, and that allows them to reflect on how they manage their emotions. She has had children tell her that when they get anxious or angry they think of Mole and all he has been through. They know that Mole is a good boy, and that they are too.

It's almost as if everybody on the yard has a story, including Carrie herself. What she went through with her fall was incredibly difficult psychologically, but there is strength in the very struggle. Sometimes she finds that even the scars on her arms from her operations can open up conversations, particularly with children, about what it means to not have the perfect body, or about self-harm.

What's really important to Carrie is that everyone who comes to the yard for one of her courses is treated like an individual, with their own individual needs: 'It's their story, it's their life, it's what they're working on. To watch that progression is supercool.' Carrie remembers in particular an emergency worker who she matched with a pony that was hypervigilant and extremely wary of men. Carrie had to explain to him at the beginning of the course that it was likely to take the full six weeks to gain Porridge's trust. He would have to be calm; he may well have to deal with some steps backward without getting too disheartened, and he would have to keep trying. Like life, this wasn't going to be easy. But by the end of the course, the pony was shoulder to shoulder with him, nuzzling his side in a gesture of total confidence. The bond between them, he said, was 'spiritual'. You could see the pride and openness shine out of his face. 'That pony changed that man's life,' says Carrie.

'It's a privilege to witness the life-changing things that happen out there,' she adds. Watching a child who has been on the verge of exclusion from school beam as he receives his certificate, or friendships blossom among veterans who had closed themselves off from the world, or smiles returning to the face of a woman who has been through domestic violence is all the reward Carrie needs. For her, what they do isn't overly complicated: 'It's about bringing joy and light into peoples' lives, because mental health has often got such a black cloud associated with it, and rightly so, because depression and anxiety and stress are hard. But it's all about finding the joy.'

★

The pandemic was a huge challenge for the charity, not least financially. 'But we're not beaten by stuff here,' says Carrie, so on the first day of the first lockdown in March 2020 she did a huge call around to find out what all the support services were doing. Most were having to close their doors, but Carrie thought it over and reckoned that they could do more because as an open-air facility they could keep going within government guidelines. She knew that the lockdown was going to put more people into crisis – children going through bereavement, military veterans who would not be able to handle being constrained by lockdown, NHS workers whose jobs were unimaginably stressful. 'So we just made a plan. We're more a team of what we *can* do, not what we're limited by, so we highlighted the people who really really needed us and made a plan based on that.' Carrie is matter-of-fact as she describes this, but the challenge of keeping even the riding stables itself going – the expense of feeding the horses, the worry about the team, the stress of the stories she was hearing from the course participants – must have been huge. How did she get through it? 'We kept on going, kept outside and kept busy, really.'

Stable Lives as a charity is entirely a voluntary organisation: the staff at the riding school contribute their time for free, and all the running of the charity is done, unpaid, by Carrie herself, with some family support. 'I need to work on that, actually,' she says with a laugh. There is always another fundraising venture to tackle (since her 24-hour ride she has also organised a 24-hour stretcher carry, and completed Tough Mudder). She has written children's books inspired by the horses in the yards, she goes into schools to talk to children about mental health, she puts on nativity concerts and somehow in there also finds time for her family.

There's always another horizon for Carrie: her dream is that the Stable Lives model could be rolled out across the country and beyond, into as many riding schools and stable yards as possible. She knows the programme is simple and effective enough that it could be transplanted into any establishment where the staff were willing, because as far as she is concerned it is the animals that are doing the teaching; she is just a facilitator. To me, that sounds like part and parcel of her natural modesty: 'The ponies do the work. I just present some workshops and then throw a pony or a dog in and they get on with it... I just think animals are amazing.'

But I think most of us would agree that the really amazing ingredient is Carrie herself.

Heather Bryson

Let me tell you about Heather Bryson. She's a ten-year-old girl with curly red hair, an enormous smile and absolutely buckets of energy. She also has a huge heart, which was really the reason I came across her in the first place, when she was nominated as a Young Loneliness Champion for *Good Morning Britain*'s 1 Million Minutes campaign. When I saw what she had been doing during the pandemic, I could understand why: her fitness videos, aimed at people in care homes with dementia, had gone viral, helping so many elderly people whose lives had been so affected by Covid. This little girl was using her time, creativity and energy to make a real difference to people.

It all started in lockdown. Talking to Heather now, all excitement and cheeky wit, it is extraordinary to hear from her mother Deborah that when the pandemic hit, eight-year-old Heather became really depressed. Deborah watched in horror as her 'bubbly wee girl' disappeared, retreating into herself.

Reaching for what they knew she loved – arts and crafts – her parents soon discovered that this was a pathway not just to helping her, but also others. Heather at first found a focus making birdfeeders out of recycled cups; she also made what she called 'lockdown angels' – beautiful beaded pendants – from broken necklaces. But for someone like Heather, just making things wasn't enough. Soon she was selling all of her creations at a craft fair to raise money for Alzheimer Scotland.

Another way she started reaching out was within her own family – doing chair exercises over Zoom with her grandmother, who was in a care home. It turned out that all her granny's friends wanted to do this too, so Heather found herself doing exercise classes with them all. Sadly, Heather's grandmother died during lockdown, and like so many others across the country Heather was unable to say goodbye to her properly.

The idea was born to make the chair exercises she had been doing with her granny accessible to more people by making them into videos and putting them on YouTube so that care homes could access them free of charge. This wasn't an easy undertaking: Heather knew she had to be careful because a lot of the people she was reaching out to might have restricted mobility or other needs, so the first step was a lot of research to find out what exercises were safe and suitable. Luckily her mum works for Alzheimer Scotland, so that was the first port of call – Deborah reached out through them to NHS physiotherapists who gave Heather the information she needed. It was all about simple exercises that could be done in a chair – arm stretches, gentle leg and foot exercises, seated marching, seated rowing.

By now, the whole family found themselves on a learning curve. Heather's dad Gary became the videographer. His background in training helped to structure the videos, to make them as user friendly as possible, adding music and learning about the software as he went along. Meanwhile, Deborah had to give herself a crash course in social media: she discovered that Facebook had a great community of care home activity co-ordinators, and this turned out to be a fantastic way to get the videos seen by the people who needed them.

But the star of the videos was, of course, Heather. If you watch them, you will see that she takes her role very seriously: the exercise is the main point here, and Heather is very sober, clear and calm when demonstrating them. She can't help her cheeky grin coming across when she's introducing them though! In her trainers and leggings, she is just sunshine in a bottle: you can see why her videos have become so popular.

The family's efforts got a reception they could never have predicted. Heather's first video on her YouTube channel received more than 2,000 hits within 24 hours. On 11th June 2021, she did a special live event as part of the Captain Tom 100 event in memory of her hero, Captain Tom Moore. For this, she challenged herself to do a live broadcast into 100 care homes round the world at the same time. It was something that was in fact a challenge for the whole family: it wasn't easy to set up and perform, but they pulled it off. As Deborah puts it, 'It's just getting bigger and bigger and bigger.' She has people who tune into her videos from as far afield as Australia, Singapore, New Zealand and America. She has even been recognised by fellow holidaymakers when she was away in Turkey.

This was what led to her Young Loneliness Champion nomination. Anyone who was watching *Good Morning Britain* on the morning we spoke to her will remember her astonishment when her hero, Joe Wicks, came on virtually to meet her, and her cry of 'Daddy, Daddy, I've won it!'

So I was interested to talk to Heather a few months later and discover what she had been up to since. It wasn't a surprise to find she hadn't been sitting back and resting on her laurels: her videos are becoming even more accessible, through a platform which provides resources for care home residents. The thing that was really firing her up though was the fact that she was doing something special for the Queen's Jubilee, in association with the Scouts, with St Andrew's First Aid and with the Royal Lifeguards (Heather is a rookie lifeguard herself). This event was all about the generations pulling together, something Heather really embodies. To me, this is the most impressive thing about what Heather did: she thought about people who were in such a different situation to her, and she found such a simple, practical way to help and connect with them. We all know how hard Covid and the lockdowns hit people living in care homes; it's terrible to think of the isolation they went through. How fantastic that a young girl found a way to inject a bit of cheer and sunshine into their days.

Heather's exercise videos and crafts are not the only way she helps people – almost as an aside, she tells me that she also does volunteering work for an organisation called The Sporting Aces, which helps children who have learning difficulties or physical challenges participate in sports. Heather will act as a guide for those with visual impairments, or help those with mobility problems. At Easter, the family went into a care home to give out Easter eggs and have a singsong and a session. At Christmas, they dressed as elves for charity. Anything to raise money and raise a smile.

Heather is extraordinary, not just for what she has done at such a young age but for the joy and enthusiasm with which she does it. Her motto is 'Thumbs up and smile!' and you can see that smile has been reflected back at her from so many people. But what is interesting is how much she herself has got out of all the effort she puts out there. The depression she suffered under lockdown has gone, her bubbly confidence is back. Having had to move schools at one point to a much bigger school – it was 'sink or swim!' as her mother says – within five weeks she was made a junior house captain. Her life is so different from the depressed little girl of a few years ago, and she has learned a huge lesson from all of this: what makes other people happy makes you happy, and if you can go out there and spread some smiles it might lift your mood, too.

For Heather and her whole family, it isn't just about raising the money, or even about raising awareness: it's about giving some of your time, about helping people. As a family, the message they want to share is that if they can do it, anyone can: 'We are finding our way, if we can keep learning then so can everybody else.' And as for Heather, what does she feel when she sees the effects of all her efforts, and how she has brightened other people's days? The answer is simple: 'Happy!'

Jem Stein

My next humble hero proves the innovative power of a simple but brilliant idea. That is, if you marry it to a serious drive and the ability to get things done.

The problem first presented itself to Jem Stein while he was still at university and took part in a befriending scheme for refugees. He was paired with a boy called Adam, who had fled from Darfur aged just sixteen, leaving behind everything that was familiar to him. On arrival in the UK, he claimed refugee status as an asylum seeker. What this meant, legally, is that that while Adam was waiting for his status to be decided, he was housed – in his case right on the outskirts of London near Heathrow airport – and he was allowed a stipend of £38 per week (at the time of writing it is £40.85). And that was it. He was not allowed to work or claim any other benefits. In other words, he had just £38 per week to cover food, clothing, medicine and of course transport. Asylum seekers will typically be in this limbo for six months at the very least while their claim is processed – usually longer. All of which means that getting around – to access education, or healthcare, or legal advice, or support, let alone any kind of social connection – becomes almost impossible in a city like London where a bus pass costs £21 a week. It meant that Adam could barely participate in the befriending scheme that Jem had joined. Jem solved this problem by getting hold of an old bike, so that Adam could have some means of going from place to place. It opened his life up. 'That was really the first step into normal living for him,' says Jem.

It sounds a bit like an old riddle – when is a bike not a bike? When it's a whole lot more than that: it's the freedom to be more independent, to make connections, to go beyond the confines of your neighbourhood, to start participating in society. If an asylum seeker is eventually granted refugee status, it's also a way to access interviews and employment. Not to mention the very well-attested physical and mental health benefits of cycling – if you're someone like me who really needs to keep exercising and who definitely feels cooped up if they can't get out there, you'll really appreciate the difference that a bike can make.

Seeing how much the gift of one simple bike had helped Adam was a lesson that stayed with Jem, and when he left university he decided to try and do the same for other asylum seekers. The stroke of genius was realising how many unused bikes there are. In London alone, according to Transport for London, 270,000 bikes are abandoned every year, and that figure doesn't even count those bikes that are sitting unused in garden sheds or rusting away in people's garages. Between 20,000 and 40,000 refugees arrive in this country every year;

imagine how fantastic it would be to match the demand to this oversupply. So Jem's idea was this: get people to donate bikes, refurbish them, and pass them on to asylum seekers and refugees. At first, he did this in his spare time, and then in 2013 he took the plunge, left his job, and set up The Bike Project as a charity.

It was one of those brilliant ideas that involves quite a lot of hard work to organise. Starting off by asking for donations, the first thing Jem discovered was that there was a huge willingness to donate. 'People like the idea that their old rusty bike might go to a good cause,' he says. To some extent, he was often solving a problem for them by taking their awkward old bikes off their hands. In the early days he would just rent a van, pick up the bikes from people's homes, and store them in a cupboard under the stairs in a council estate in Hackney. To start off with, the refurbishing was done in a tiny workshop, moving to a much bigger one as the charity grew. Jem himself trained as a bike mechanic as soon as he had quit his job, only to discover that that was definitely not where his talents lay. 'I'm the joke of the workshop – they all get worried if they see me pick up a spanner,' he says.

Quite quickly, demand started to grow to match the supply. In the early days, people would come on a Thursday – which was their session to give out bikes – and pretty much every week the number of people arriving would more or less match the number of bikes they had to give out. That is until word began to get out, and suddenly one day, says Jem, 'There were queues round the block and no system to keep people's names.' People who had travelled to get to them were naturally upset – 'It was complete chaos' – an early lesson in how you can be a victim of your own success. On the hoof, they had to come up with a system to manage a waiting list. Ever since, they have found that growth has been their main challenge: while it might sound a simple notion to take old bikes and pass them on to those who need them, there are a lot of moving parts to the operation. From refurbishing the bikes and obtaining spare parts, keeping track of their stock and the potential demand to managing overheads and keeping track of volunteers. With all these demands on his time and energy, it's possibly a good thing that Jem is not a talented enough mechanic to be on the floor of the workshop.

Nowadays, The Bike Project has projects in six different cities and employs 43 people. Asylum seekers and refugees are typically referred on to them by the big charities and organisations, or sometimes hear of them by word of mouth. Of the bikes donated, they match two-thirds with the people who need them, and raise the money to keep going both from direct donations and by selling the remaining third. Over the first years, the growth of both supply and demand was steady – in that first year they gave away 120 bikes; it has gone up every year since and they are looking at donating over 3,000 bikes this year. In all, they have given more than 9,000 bikes to refugees in need.

Not only that, but the charity goes far beyond simply giving out bicycles. Realising how many refugee women in particular weren't able to ride bikes, the charity set up Pedal Power – free cycling lessons for women, given by women. Needless to say, as well as the ability to cycle, this is also furnishing these women with confidence, connections, a level of freedom. Continuing the theme, the Bike Buddies scheme the charity runs matches up volunteers with asylum seekers to go cycling with. It's not hard to see the benefits that brings: socialisation, exercise, human interaction. Refugees are also encouraged to volunteer with the charity itself, improving their skills and giving them a purpose. These bikes are a lot more than just two wheels and a handlebar!

The real mushrooming of the charity came in 2020 with the advent of the pandemic. Because cycling was one of the few activities not curtailed by lockdowns, the demand for bikes on the sales side took off, just at the time when logistics and refurbishment became that much more complicated. Naturally, it was fantastic to be able to help more and more people, but Jem has definitely found it comes with its own issues – the infrastructure you build for an organisation to give away a few hundred bikes a year has to change quite radically once you're giving away thousands across half a dozen cities. And of course lockdowns made some of the face-to-face schemes the charity was running impossible. Nevertheless, The Bike Project rallied and did what it could online, setting up Cyber Cyclist, online activities over Zoom so that people could access cycling-themed exercise, films and education. 'It's been a rollercoaster,' says Jem, with what I suspect is huge understatement.

When the charity started in 2013, Jem was often met with a slightly baffled reaction, as though people didn't really realise that there were asylum seekers in the country. The increased visibility of the refugee cause, fuelled by the successive crises of Syria and Afghanistan (and now Ukraine), had already raised the profile of the charity and the desire to donate. Now, world events and the news agenda have pushed the refugee cause to the top of the national consciousness, often in the most contentious of ways. It would be easy to get a very skewed impression of how many asylum seekers are coming, and what they receive when they get here. In fact, refugees make up a tiny proportion of the population – just 0.2 per cent – but that is still a lot of lives having to be lived in the most difficult of circumstances. And as debate rages, the needs of the asylum seekers do not change.

The charity is now giving out bikes to every age group – from young children to people in their seventies. In fact, the demand for children's bikes is increasing all the time as more and more families arrive. Just think of the difference a bike might make to a child who has arrived on these shores through the trauma of war, and the kinds of journeys they have endured: the contrast between that and the kind of journeys that they can now enjoy on two wheels, filled with laughter and a sense of freedom. The simple joy of getting on a bike must be transformative.

Jem describes himself as a 'glass half empty' person, always thinking about what more he could have done, and what he can do in the future. Still, there are definitely moments when the human value of what he has done is brought home to him in technicolour. Like the moment when a talented marathon runner got in touch: he was running in professional races, and wanted to be 'sponsored' by The Bike Project. It wasn't that he wanted any money, he just wanted to display their logo on his kit, as a gesture of thanks for the bike they had given him when he was a refugee six years before.

Hassan Akkad, the BAFTA-winning filmmaker and Syrian refugee – an amazing hero himself – is another person who has been helped along the way by a Bike Project bike. There are other refugees who have been recipients of bikes, have volunteered and gone on to become involved with the charity itself. What a fantastic way to make people feel like they belong – helping them to help others. Being an ambitious type, Jem wants to do even more with the charity: in particular, they are working on an online platform that will allow recipients of bikes to connect with each other in a Bike Project community. And he has a vision of what he would like the future to be – one where they are able to offer a bike to every asylum seeker as soon as they arrive in this country. 'We're still a bit of a way off that,' he says, but given his brilliance and focus, I will not be surprised if he gets there.

The Bike Project cannot hope to solve every problem that comes with being an asylum seeker or refugee. These are people undergoing the toughest of experiences, who have left behind everything they hold dear and who are making their way in a foreign place where it must sometimes seem the system is stacked against them. There is no magic wand here. But in looking at one very specific practical need, The Bike Project is addressing a whole lot more than just a transport issue. It is doing what it can to provide freedom, community and, I hope, a sense of welcome.

Vicky Hogg

I think Vicky Hogg is actually a hero on two counts. The first is simply her job: in everyday life Vicky is a carer in the local community in Doncaster. Most of her work involves looking after elderly people, especially those with dementia. It's a job she has loved since she first went to work in a care home, following in the footsteps of her mother, who is also a carer. Vicky fell in love with the job 'from the moment she stepped through the door' and now she works for the local authority in a caring role within the community.

I think we all know that being a carer is one of the most incredibly important roles there can be. If like me you've seen up close the support and help that carers can bring to any individual or family living with dementia then you'll know it can be absolutely invaluable. You'll probably also agree that this job is both incredibly demanding and often underappreciated. Just to have a calm, helpful professional presence there and on your side can do such a power of good to people going through the worst of times, and having had the good fortune to meet the fantastic Vicky, who just radiates warmth and happiness, I have no doubt that she brings a bit of sunshine to all her clients.

She loves to do the job, she tells me, just to give something back to people who have worked hard themselves their whole lives. During the pandemic, of course, the role became even tougher and even more necessary – Vicky and her colleagues found they were having to go knock on doors in their own time to make sure their clients were getting by. It was heartbreaking for her to witness the isolation they were going through, and though she wears it lightly, my guess is it was a pretty scary time for everyone in her profession. So I'd love to award her 'humble hero' status purely as a representative of every person in the country who puts their all into caring work.

★

But in fact, brilliant as all that is, being a carer is not the reason that multiple people nominated Vicky when I put out a call for humble heroes on social media. Those nominations came because of the fantastic work she has done raising money for charities through the crazy endurance challenges she puts herself through. Most of the people who nominated her said something along the lines of: 'She puts her body through hell just to raise money for charity', and looking at the feats she has accomplished, I would totally agree.

Actually, it's hilarious talking to Vicky, because she talks about these extreme challenges in such a casual way. She has always loved sport ever since she was a little girl, and having done a few 'little things' already – that's 'little things' like marathons and half marathons – she thought she'd like to challenge herself a bit more and be a bit adventurous. So she asked some friends if they fancied cycling with her from John O'Groats to Land's End for charity, and they said, 'Why not?' I love that spirit: 'Let's just do something mad and fantastic just to help other people': which is exactly what Vicky and her friends did.

That challenge meant that she had to cycle 100 miles a day for 12 days. It was painful, but great fun, says Vicky, and apart from raising money for charity (in this case the Sick Children's Trust), it gave her the bug to want to do more and bigger things. So, after doing a run from Whitehaven to Sunderland in 2020, the following year she went for a really big one. This time she wouldn't just cycle the length of the country: she would do it on foot. 'I just thought, well, I've cycled it, now I can run it.'

Now, as I know to my cost from the things Ivan has roped me into, running that kind of distance is a very different proposition to cycling. (Not least because at least on a bike you get a bit of a rest on the downhills.) To do it all on your own two feet, nothing to help you power through the miles, is quite something. ('Oh, the blisters: it was crazy,' says Vicky.) It took 30 days, doing 30 miles – that's more than a marathon – every single day with no days off. She was supported by a few friends driving her van, and to listen to her you'd think it was the simplest thing in the world: 'We just went the whole way together' is how she describes it.

Not that it didn't have its moments: at one point the van broke down when there was just one person driving it, threatening to leave them stranded. There were days when she had to cut her toenails off to be able to get her trainers on, or when getting out of bed to get going was almost impossible.

But even the difficulties she faced sometimes ended up being a positive: when her knees started to hurt she put out a call on social media and was bowled over by the offers of help she got from physios offering her free treatment to help her on her way. These were people she had never met before, who were so inspired by her efforts that they wanted to get involved, and who now have become friends purely because of their willingness to do what they could. It's a really lovely illustration of something I've noticed when talking to all the humble heroes I've met: the more they put good things out into the world, the more they see good reflected back at them.

On that run from John O'Groats to Land's End Vicky was raising money for Dementia UK – inspired of course by her work. For her, it wasn't just about the money raised, it was a question of her wanting to give that bit more to people who are going through one of the hardest things life can throw at you. Those people were at the forefront of her mind as she ran: 'I couldn't wait to tell people as I'm going down the country what I'm doing and why I'm doing it.' That was what inspired her to keep pushing on. She reminds me a lot of Ivan when she explains how the thought of the people she was helping kept powering her legs through the worst of the exhaustion. 'Me putting myself through that little bit of pain for a month is nothing compared to people who have to go through that every day.'

Like Ivan, she knows too that the mental battle is more important than the physical one: 'If you can control your mind, and your thoughts, and the pain you're in, then your body will keep going'. It helps that, as she freely admits, she's a little bit addicted to the buzz of it: the mixture of adventure and the fact that she's helping as many people as she can. That's why she likes to pick a different charity each time, so that she can spread both the awareness and the fundraising across as many causes as possible.

★

Whenever I've done any physical challenges, one question that I always get is: 'What are you going to do next?' People tend to ask you this about five minutes after you cross the finish line, and I never know what to say; just let me catch my breath a minute here. Vicky, though, is the absolute opposite. She loves coming up with new challenges, and in fact she does while she's running the current one. 'When I'm doing the challenges I'm always thinking, How can I push myself a little bit more? Who can I help next?' I guess that's the difference between someone like Vicky and me, and it's what makes her a proper hero.

So it's not a surprise when I ask Vicky that question and discover that she has come up with something even more challenging. She's calling this one the Wales 400, and it will involve running the length of Wales, then walking the whole of the Anglesey Coastal Path, and then climbing mountains Tryfan and Snowdon: the challenge will end on the peak. It's 400 miles over 14 days, which sounds hard enough – the terrain is going to be incredibly steep in places – but the challenge here is that for the first time she will be doing it totally unsupported. In other words, she'll be carrying everything she needs on her back. I'm excited to find out how she gets on. I'm pretty sure that she will be doing it with a smile on her face.

I know the kind of stamina, and also the planning, that has to go into the kind of challenge that Vicky does. And yet she wears it so lightly – to talk to her, you'd think it was the easiest thing in the world to embark on. So I'm curious about what she would say to anyone else who fancies putting themselves through this to raise money. Do you have to be super-fit and super-strong? Her answer is immediate, and typical: 'I am so not that person. I'm not really a runner, I'm just an average Joe. I always say you only fail if you don't try. If you try, as long as you try, it doesn't matter.'

My guess is that Vicky won't stop trying anytime soon, and will be doing good and spreading her own brand of cheerful positivity for a long time to come.

Harry Moseley

It's not often you meet someone who changes your point of view. It's even more surprising if that person is a nine-year-old child.

I first met Harry Moseley in 2009 at an event to raise money for the Seve Ballesteros Foundation. I was hosting, and Harry was giving a speech. This was in front of 2,000 people, and no usual audience either: the crowd included celebrities – sportsmen and women, elite athletes, the works. Harry meanwhile was a young schoolboy from the Midlands, who had come along with his mum Georgie. He was talking to us about brain cancer. Having been diagnosed with an inoperable brain tumour at the age of seven, he had turned the fight against cancer into his personal mission.

Meeting him was a moment I'll never forget: his wide smile and bright eyes lit up the stage. He spoke to us about his efforts to raise money and awareness of brain cancer (and, by the way, his efforts that day helped raise £53,000 for the

Foundation). Remarkably, he wasn't doing this because of his own illness: he had been inspired by his friendship with a fellow patient at the Queen Elizabeth Hospital, a man in his fifties called Robert Harley.

Like Harry, Robert was suffering with a brain tumour, and the two of them had struck up an unlikely friendship across the generations. Most of Harry's treatments had been at a children's hospital, but his radiotherapy had been at the Queen Elizabeth Hospital in Birmingham, where there were patients of all ages undergoing the same treatment. Harry's treatment meant coming in every day for thirty days, so for someone as gregarious as Harry, it was a natural opportunity to get talking. One of the other patients was Robert, and the two of them got on famously. On Harry's final day of treatment, he brought in gifts – little angel keyrings – and cards for the other patients. In return, Robert gave Harry his business card, and when they finished their radiography treatments they kept in touch. Their check-up scans would often fall on the same day, so Harry would ring Robert the night before to wish him luck. After a while, Robert invited Harry and his family to visit his farm. It was a joy-filled day. They rode together in one of many of Robert's vintage cars – Harry perched up on the back, beaming from ear to ear. He loved having the chance to introduce Robert to his sister Dani and brother Louie, who had heard so much about him. And he got the chance to visit Robert's office – he was a director of a big company – and sit on his office chair. He loved all that, and was fascinated by the business. But this visit marked one of the last moments before Robert's condition deteriorated. Not long after, Georgie received a call from Robert's wife to say that he was in hospital. Harry was insistent that he wanted to go and visit, something that his mum and dad were naturally very cautious about – Harry was only eight, and they felt that with Robert having the same condition as Harry, seeing him so ill was too close to home for such a young boy. Harry's words when this was explained to him are just so characteristic of the kind of person he was: 'Mum,' he said, 'I know you don't want me to be sad, but if I was poorly, you wouldn't want people not to come and see me because of how they felt.'

So Harry made the visit. Robert was mostly asleep, but Harry talked to him throughout, telling him that when he came home Harry would come and help look after him and make him better. At one point Robert turned to him and whispered, 'That would be lovely.' Think how frightening it must have been for Harry – to see someone he was close to go through this ordeal, and to know that it was possible that he was on the same path. But Robert was his friend, and he wanted to bring him comfort. On the way home he was quiet, eventually breaking his silence to say, 'I've got to do something. There's not enough being done to help people with cancer.' But he didn't know what he could do.

The next day, to take his mind off things, Georgie took him to Hobbycraft – he loved making things. As they walked round, he suddenly spotted a shelf of coloured beads and, says Georgie, 'his little face – I can see it now – just beamed, and he said, "That's it!"' His idea was to make plastic beaded bracelets and sell them to raise some money to go towards cancer charities. At the time there was a fashion of wearing rubber bracelets for charitable causes, but Harry loved the idea of beading bracelets instead. He could make them in any colours the customer wanted, and they would fit anybody: adult or child, girl or boy. He took the beads home, and he and his brother and sister spent a day in the garden making the first bracelets. Harry took it really seriously, coming up with a name – Help Harry Help Others – and enlisting Georgie's friend Sarah, a designer, to help design a logo. (Harry specified that the colours should all be happy ones.)

His campaign started small – he thought he would sell his bracelets to friends and family – but it wasn't long before this just wasn't enough for Harry. He wanted to reach wider, get more people involved. So he developed a programme which allowed him to go into schools, to talk about his condition and raise awareness. He would take in his beads and elastic and all the bits they would need to make bracelets. Then he would sell the products to the pupils, for them to make into bracelets and sell themselves for charities that were important to them. It was a business school – engage the kids in the idea, sell it to them, allow them to make the products, and make money for the charities that they cared about.

The heart-wrenching thing was that just as Harry started on this journey, Robert died. It was clear that this hugely affected Harry, but he didn't let it stop him, and by the time I met him he was confident enough to go onstage in front of all those people and tell his story. The event was intimidating enough for me as the host, and it's my job to stand up in front of an audience and speak. This young boy had to go up there and talk about the really tough stuff – his own illness, his friend's death. How on earth did Harry deal with the nerves?

'Oh that's easy,' he said with a glint in his eye, a glint I would come to know very well. 'I imagine them all sitting on the loo!' What was apparent from the moment we met was that we would get on like a house on fire, and sure enough I had the most brilliant evening in the company of this joyous, charismatic, fun and cheeky boy.

I woke up the next day very early for work to find that Harry had left me a note: 'Hi Ben, here's my mum's number to stay in touch. It was great to meet you. Harry. PS save some of the girls for me!' Did I mention he was really cheeky?

The next time I saw Harry was at quite a momentous occasion: a special launch for Help Harry Help Others. The launch was quite an intimate event that was held at a hotel in west London. Harry was in raring form. I went up to say hi to him and Georgie when I arrived.

'Hi mate,' I said, and he grinned up at me with his cheerful round face and glasses.

'Hi Georgie,' I said to his mum, giving her a hug. 'You're looking fantastic.'

'You what?' interrupted Harry, looking incredulous. And without missing a beat he whipped his glasses off and handed them to me. 'I think you need these, mate,' he said.

He had been to Hamleys that day and bought one of those coin tricks – a little box where you put in a stack of coins and shake it, and then when you open it all the coins have gone. He loved this trick and was showing it to everyone. This was quite up my street, so I showed him this very simple coin trick that I know: you take a 20-pence coin in each hand and flip them over, and when you open your hands one of the coins has 'disappeared'. (It's a question of flicking the coin very quickly into the other hand, and you can't see it as long as you practise the movement enough.) Harry was just made up with this trick, and spent the whole time, all through this posh launch, flicking his hands and perfecting it.

That's what I loved about Harry: he was just a little boy in so many ways. With most children, what's important to them in the moment is the toy they are playing with, the programme they are watching, the sweets they might be allowed later. They think the world revolves around them. And that's what we want – we want them to smile and enjoy life and to learn, and not to worry about others. But you could sense with Harry, he'd be playing his tricks and cheeking his mum like any quick-witted kid, but he also had this innate sense that actually life wasn't all about him: life was about other people.

As Georgie says now, Harry had no concept when he made his first bracelet of the opportunities that would come from that. He would end up talking to politicians at the House of Commons, meeting the England football team, who backed his campaign, and receiving all sorts of awards. He was named as Britain's Kindest Kid, for which he visited 10 Downing Street, and given the Children's Champion Award, which took him to Buckingham Palace. His message reached far and wide, with an amazing range of supporters. For him, all those moments were about the awareness and money he could raise for the cause. 'He just wanted to fix things,' says his mum, 'I always say that Harry proved that regardless of your age, your wealth, your lifestyle or your wellbeing, you can achieve anything if you are passionate enough.'*

Whatever Harry was facing – the illness, the pain and headaches he would experience, the frustration, the fact that he couldn't be at school with his friends – he never allowed anything to hold him back. His aim was to improve the lives of others who were struggling with cancer, and he focused on that with all the energy he had. Everything he did was for other people. He always used to say he wasn't interested in telling us about how he was feeling, because he didn't want people to feel sorry for him. All he wanted was to share positivity and happiness.

In 2011 the headaches Harry had been suffering from worsened, and it became clear that the tumour had grown. Though it had previously been inoperable due to its position in his brain, there was now a possibility that its very growth had made it partly accessible. There was nothing for it but to operate, or the tumour would kill him, but it was a highly dangerous operation that Harry underwent on 8th August 2011. I don't like to think about what his family must have gone through as he went into surgery. And I can't bear how it must have felt for them when the worst happened, and a haemorrhage during the operation meant that he went into a coma.

Harry had a huge Twitter following – around 100,000 followers, which was enormous for a young boy – and there was a huge upswelling of emotion focused around the hashtag #wakeupHarry. He would have loved that – he really enjoyed the interaction that he had with people on Twitter (he called it his 'Twitfam'), and he had built this huge following just by being his unique and authentic self – but I don't know if he would really have understood the scale of that outpouring of love and hope for him.

It wasn't enough. He never woke up. After 14 weeks they allowed him to leave hospital so that he could be at home at the end, in accordance with his wishes, and it was there that they turned off the ventilator and he died in Georgie's arms, just as she had promised. It's hard to think that all that hope and joy and childlike fun was extinguished in that moment.

I've never seen anything like Harry's funeral. Georgie had kindly invited me and the entrepreneur and philanthropist Duncan Bannatyne – who was a big supporter of Harry's and admired his business sense – to the house beforehand. I felt a great sense of trepidation as we approached. I wanted to be there and to pay my respects, but I was also very conscious that I didn't want to intrude on the family at this very, very personal time. The house was of course full of family, and the welcome we got from them cut through any discomfort I might have felt, but it was strange to feel such a sombre atmosphere in a place you knew Harry had lit up for so long. Georgie hugged me, and then brought me into the room to where Harry was lying in his coffin. All that energy, stilled. It was a moment I shall never forget; it was like nothing I had experienced before. I was grateful to have the chance to connect with him at some level, to say goodbye and tell him how peaceful he looked. But even though his death hadn't been unexpected, and his body was right there in front of me, it was hard to comprehend.

From the stillness and quiet of the house, we drove through the town to the church. And it was that drive that really brought home what Harry had achieved. As the procession moved through the town, spontaneous applause broke out from people on the street, because they knew what it was. Every street the cortège turned down, people stopped and started clapping, and as we approached the church the crowds got larger and larger. Getting out of the car the wave of emotion felt extraordinary. It was something really special, almost exciting – as though Harry was a rockstar. It sounds strange to describe it like that, but I knew Harry would have loved to have seen it – he loved being the centre of attention. It was overwhelming to think about the impact this kid had had in such a short space of time. He was so well known locally that thousands of people had come out just to stand outside for the ceremony, because the church itself was absolutely rammed. It was a big church, and walking in and taking the scale of it in was remarkable. It felt like some kind of state funeral – the service full of pomp and ceremony, the formal dark suits of the mourners enlivened by the bright yellow flowers the family had asked us to wear.

And through the sadness I couldn't help but give a wry smile, because of a brilliant Harry juxtaposition: right at the heart of all the grandeur, all the respect and impressive crowds and love and elegance, was this ridiculously garish bright blue SpongeBob SquarePants coffin. And that was Harry all over: he just had a way of cutting through. So you can adhere to social etiquette and be brilliant and selfless and brave in your life and do amazing things, but you can also be cheeky. And there he was among the formality, still drawing attention and making people smile. Even at this most sombre of moments Harry was shining his bright, colourful light for us all.

Harry's death was a horrific ordeal for his family, and especially his mum. Georgie had been a rock to Harry throughout everything. If he was a hero to others, she was most definitely a heroine to him. Throughout all she had had to shoulder with Harry's illness, she had done everything she could to support his mission. She was the person he looked up to most, and she was consistently amazed by everything he did. Now there was a gaping hole.

★

What Georgie did next is testament to what a wonderful team they made, and how precious her son was. At first, she didn't know if she could carry on the charity, heartbroken as she was. 'And then I just thought, you know what? Cancer can never take away from me that I will always be Harry's mummy, and I still support his dreams and will do for as long as I can.' Harry's dream had been the charity, so Georgie poured her grief and love into furthering its reach by setting up the Help Harry Help Others cancer centre. This is a charity providing help with all things related to the trauma of watching a family member going through cancer. Nobody knew better than Georgie how hard times can be for a family going through this. Everyone in that family knew that cancer is a disease that affects more than just the sufferer themselves.

The Help Harry Help Others cancer centre is still going strong, providing support to those who need it most. The charity donates to research into brain cancers; it gives grants to families suffering financial hardship; it has volunteers on hand to help with everything from wigs to counselling, benefits and housing advice, and general emotional support. All of this because a young boy wanted to do something practical to help his friend.

Harry was eleven when he lost his battle, but he'd done so much in that time. He'd raised over £750,000 through his charity. A huge sum, but you can't measure what Harry achieved in pounds and pence. By sheer force of personality, he had brought celebrities on board to raise the profile of brain cancer. Most of all, he inspired thousands of kids, introducing them to the idea of fundraising and engaging them in business ideas and moneymaking. This was social enterprise, well before it became a buzzword. Harry was years ahead of his time, and that was the one thing he didn't have.

★

I said at the outset that Harry had changed the way I think about the world. What do I mean by that? For me, he represents what true selflessness can look like. I remember once he was on a TV show where he was taken to meet Father Christmas in Lapland. They were asked to write a letter to Father Christmas to ask what present he would like. Harry's answer? That all he wanted was a cure for brain tumours so that other people wouldn't have to suffer. (Though since that probably wasn't possible, he wouldn't mind a bike.) He wasn't saying this for effect. It was just who he was, in the fabric of his DNA. He had this extraordinary way of automatically thinking about others – that's what all his warmth and his charm were about. As his mum puts it: 'I think it was just he had an amazing positive outlook. I wish we could all see through Harry's glasses... unless he was telling jokes about me!' There are very few people who are like that even as adults, but Harry just had this light inside him. He realised he had an opportunity to make people feel better, whether they were unhappy, ill or hurting, and I think that made him feel better himself. He gathered a lot of happiness from being able to spread that love and support. To him, it was fun. I think sometimes we think of selflessness as overly noble and dour, or self-sacrificing in some way. But Harry showed me that it can be joy-filled and creative. Georgie says it best: 'If there were a million Harrys in the world, wouldn't it be a much nicer place? I wish we could programme everyone to be like Harry.'

Harry would be 21 now, and I often catch myself thinking about him – the texts he used to send me, the warmth of the hugs I would see him giving his mother, his grin after he'd come up with some cheeky riposte, the way he could charm anybody in the world into buying one of his bracelets – and when I do, my first thought is not of all the money he raised, or the good deeds he did, but of the laughter. 'I don't think I have ever laughed how I laughed when Harry was on this earth,' says Georgie.

'He was a very very special character, and it does leave me thinking, how was I blessed to have Harry in my life? How was he brought to me and was he brought to me for a reason?... I always say everybody needs a Harry in their life, just to bring them perspective.' Harry showed me that no matter your own circumstances, showing up for others can be part of a life-enhancing whirlwind of fun. And for that, he will always be a hero of mine.

heroes for
change

Kwajo Tweneboa

What do you think of when you think of your home? I hope that you think of safety, of comfort, of warmth; of a place where you can be with your favourite people, gather your most precious possessions, and feel secure against the world. I hope you don't have to think of mice, cockroaches, damp, mould, asbestos. I hope that you don't have a sinking feeling every time you walk in your front door, knowing that on the other side lie ever-worsening problems that you are powerless to fix. Decent housing feels like a very, very basic need: you pay your rent, and your landlord or housing association provides a place for you to live that is safe, dry, heated and in a reasonable state of repair. But the sad reality is that in this country – the sixth richest country in the world – far too many people are having to live in conditions that are substandard, unhealthy, and in some cases even dangerous.

In May 2021 Kwajo Tweneboa, then a 22 year-old- who was working in marketing and as a teaching assistant at a school living on the Eastfields estate in Mitcham, south London, did a very simple thing that was to have extraordinarily far-reaching consequences. He took some pictures of the home that he and his sisters had been living in since the death of their father, and posted them online. The first picture was of the empty main room – walls stripped of their wallpaper, ceiling entirely ripped away to the beams, the family furniture perched outside on the balcony exposed to the elements. This was the result of a 'repair' that the landlord had started to carry out months before and which had left potentially asbestos-filled dust in its wake. The other pictures were even more shocking: in the kitchen, the ancient wooden units were falling apart because they were soaked through with damp. Throughout the flat, wallpaper was falling off the walls; holes in the plaster had been hastily and badly filled. Vermin glue traps showed evidence of serious cockroach and mice infestations. In the windowless bathroom, the only light fitting had given up a year before. On inspection, it was clear why: the whole shallow round bowl of the light fitting was filled with rainwater, pouring in from a leak above. Kwajo was having to shower at the gym. He and his family had been paying their rent and dutifully reporting the issues: whatever they did, nothing seemed to change.

Kwajo's anger was stoked by the fact that his father, a former care worker, had had to live in such poor conditions while he was dying from oesophageal cancer the year before. He had been diagnosed late 2018 and the rapid progress of the disease was terrifying. As his father wasted away, one of Kwajo's main worries had been security: with the back door and the gate on the outside fence broken, he knew that anybody who had a mind to could just walk into the house where his father was lying defenceless, bedbound and being fed by a tube. At that point, the ceiling had still been intact, but the nurses who came into the home to tend to his father had had to do their caring in the infested house, with its near-unusable kitchen and bathroom. It destroyed Kwajo to know that his father's last months had been like this.

In all of this, perhaps the worst thing was the sense of powerlessness. Again and again Kwajo complained to his housing association, Clarion. This is the largest housing association in the UK. It houses over 350,000 people and in 2020 had a turnover of about £940 million. Sometimes it seemed that it wasn't that his complaints were landing on deaf ears; it was like they simply weren't landing at all. Phone calls went unanswered. Messages, when he could leave them, were unreturned. If he finally managed to speak to anybody, it would take them ages to get back to him, or the wrong tradesmen would be sent out – that ceiling stripped to its beams in the living room? At one point they sent out roofers to deal with it. 'I thought to myself this is just completely wrong. I mean this cannot be justified, yet I am constantly complaining, complaining, complaining and being ignored.' He tried going through his MP; they were fobbed off with a letter. He got a solicitor involved, still nothing changed.

The final straw was another leak. Once again he reported it and once again days went past without action. In desperation, he decided to turn to social media. It sounds like a simple decision, but it wasn't an easy thing for him to do – these were things that he had always kept private. The sad truth was that this was not the family's first brush with substandard housing. Before this, they had been in temporary accommodation: at one point they had been housed in a mould-filled, hastily converted garage – a single room that still had the garage doors. (Kwajo's father had fought to get them into their current housing, which had only happened in 2018, less than a year before he became ill.) Kwajo knew all too well what it was like not to be able to bring friends round out of shame about what they might think, and it went against the grain to publish the state of their house to the whole world. It felt like a kind of disgrace. But it must have felt like the only resource left open to him. He took the photographs, wrote some captions, finished with 'please RT', and posted.

The response was immediate. Horrified people retweeted in droves, tagging Clarion and demanding answers. Kwajo's story was picked up by ITN, which was running an investigation into the conditions of social housing. Finally, with the weight of a huge media organisation shaming them, the housing association started to fix things that summer. They issued an apology of sorts: 'We apologise if Mr Tweneboa feels we haven't provided the service expected from us.' But for Kwajo, that was not the end of the story. Looking around his estate, he could tell even from the exteriors of the properties that his family was not the only one having to live like this. Working at a school near the estate, he began to hear stories from others who were living there that sounded very familiar – repair work not carried out, infestations of mice and cockroaches. Having finally got his own problems addressed, 'I knew that I couldn't pull the ladder up behind me when I was starting to get help.' And there was also a part of him that felt that he had a bit of a point to prove to Clarion, incensed in particular by the wording of that non-apology.

So he started to reach out to other people, leafletting every house on the estate. The response was immediate – from every corner of the estate came messages or pictures of flats in similarly dire straits. He went round and collected pictures and testimony, collating all of it into a series of posts on social media. The extent of the problem on his own doorstep surprised even Kwajo himself: the estate was rife with problems. What he found as he went round to others was that while this was going on in so many of the properties, people weren't speaking out about it. He understood why: just as he had been embarrassed to display the state of his home to the world, so were other people. Neighbours weren't speaking to each other about their mice infestations, or the fact that cockroaches were running riot across their floors. They didn't want people to know. The only people they tried to talk to about it were the landlords. And they weren't listening. But when he put it all together, the details in the stories kept repeating: mould, asbestos, damp, flooding, infestations. At one point during lockdown one child was having an online lesson when the roof above him collapsed metres from where he was sitting.

Posting those pictures, Kwajo knew he was dropping a pebble into the waters. What he didn't know what how far the ripples would spread. Or how quickly: he was at work the day he posted, and found himself running back to his friends every ten minutes, just amazed at the speed of the pickup it was getting. There were first tens and then hundreds of people picking up on it, totally aghast. 'People who had never had a clue that this sort of thing was going on were now seeing it, and were just shocked.'

That was certainly my reaction when I first saw what he

was uncovering. I was absolutely floored that in this day and age there would be people, including children and old people and people who are vulnerable, living in an environment with horrific damp, or black mould, or flooding. These were people who were paying their rent monthly, fulfilling their side of the housing contract, and yet they were having to live in conditions that were absolutely shameful. As Kwajo saw those posts gain traction, the images being shared over and over and the outrage with which people were reacting, he felt a sense of relief: 'I was thinking finally, these people are being listened to, and that was the main thing, and I was just hoping it would keep going and going and going until the CEO at the top heard. And she did.' (Not least because Kwajo started a petition later that year for her to resign from her £400,000 job.) In the wake of the furore caused by Kwajo's posts, Clarion looked into the conditions on the estate, and apologised, saying that the problems were caused because it was old housing stock reaching the end of its life, and that they were looking into regeneration. That summer, they did start to visit and make repairs.

But as Kwajo watched the reaction on his Twitter feed that day, he felt something else along with relief, because as well as the expressions of horror from people who simply did not know that people were living like this, there were also hundreds of others who saw their own experience mirrored back to them. It wasn't just that one estate in south London. He was suddenly hearing from people up and down the country who had similar issues with their housing providers. Immediately after his first thread, he discovered that within a 15-minute radius of his home there were four or five other estates where once again there were rats and mice burrowing into cupboards and running across kitchens, where leaks were unattended, and where, in one case, a woman was having to shower her children on her balcony because her shower was blocked. Horrified, he was discovering that conditions like these were rife up and down the country – the estimate is that at least 4.1 million homes in England are substandard. That is an enormous number, and it is only getting worse as our housing stock ages. But as long as it was just individuals making complaints, they couldn't make headway. These pictures though were unignorable. Within an incredibly short space of time, major news outlets were running investigations. And Kwajo realised that this was the key: with a click of a button he could reach millions of people. He could give all these people a voice, where they had been voiceless.

Since then, Kwajo has acted as a social housing superhero, answering the call of as many people who contact him about their living conditions as possible. He visits, he documents, he records the testimony from the tenants, and he posts it on Twitter. And people take notice. 'I saw that it worked and since then I haven't really stopped,' he says. Nowadays his social media is filled with pictures and videos that are frankly horrific: black mould and even mushrooms creep up the walls – in some cases it looks as though some horror-movie monster is living behind the wallpaper. Children with breathing difficulties and skin rashes abound. There are videos of water leaking through ceilings and electrical fixtures; leaks that have been left unaddressed for months on end. Raw sewage oozes from toilets onto bathroom floors, or even down walls. Frankly, no description can prepare you for the sheer weight of evidence that Kwajo has collected. The last time I looked I found myself physically recoiling from the screen at the sight of the mice squirming through a kitchen and bathroom; and I can't even bring myself to describe the infestation of enormous green spiders that one family is being forced to live with. The advice the association has given them? That they should 'Empty their shoes before putting them on.'

Perhaps even more upsetting than the images are the interviews with the tenants. Kwajo is a sensitive interviewer; he knows how difficult it is for some people to talk about all this. The terrible thing is that the stories that they tell are horribly repetitive: so many tales of people who are repeatedly ignored, funnelled through ineffective call centres, often told that the living conditions are their fault (a particularly familiar theme is to tell tenants with mould blackening their walls to the colour of soot to 'open their windows'). There are people whose doctors have written letters, advising that their living conditions are unsafe. The contrast between the extreme nature of the problems, and the casual way in which they have been dismissed or diminished defies belief.

The impact of having to live in these conditions cannot be overestimated. Kwajo himself knows only too well the mental strain it brings. People fear being judged; they worry about the health implications; their lives are made unimaginably harder in all sorts of small ways. We're talking about children who never bring friends round to their houses, about mothers who worry daily about the effect their environment is having on their children's skin or lungs, about vulnerable people left in conditions that can actively do them harm. This isn't just bricks and mortar, this is the fabric of their lives. As Kwajo points out: 'Housing associations and councils look at tenants as a nine-to-five job and then they go home at the end of the day. They don't look at it as people's lives that they are influencing and controlling and ruining.'

But the power of Kwajo's social media is starting to give them a voice. One of the most shocking videos he posted came in February 2022, when he visited a flat in Lewisham, owned by L&Q housing association, where an unbelievable infestation of cockroaches had been crawling all over the flat for a year. Glue traps were blackened with carcasses. The floor looked like it was alive (not to mention the mould which sprung from an unrepaired leak). The cockroaches were rife in the children's room. Exterminators who had been called to the flat by the landlords had refused to even enter the bedrooms. Roaches were swarming over the family as they slept, to the extent that the mother had one in her ear. The pesticides she had put down were ineffective. It was a shocking indictment. Within 24 hours of Kwajo's post appearing, it had been viewed 1 million times (the figure at the time of writing stands at 5 million). And when he emailed the CEO of L&Q with the evidence, word came back almost instantly: the family would be rehoused.

It has become a crusade. Kwajo has appeared on countless news programmes to highlight the issue. He has won awards for the work he is doing – each time drawing more publicity to the cause. He has even met with then Secretary of State Michael Gove, who made sympathetic noises and appeared to take the issue seriously. Kwajo knows he is up against a huge and seemingly inhumane system. Perhaps he cannot fix the issue one flat at a time; it is simply too big a problem on too wide a scale. But every piece of evidence he gathers, every repair done, every family rehoused, is changing perceptions. It is bringing into the light what was kept behind closed doors for too long. It is making it unignorable.

★

Back on his own estate, one neighbour who had been complaining about the unusable state of her kitchen for 27 years – longer than Kwajo has even been alive – has finally had it replaced. She's so grateful that she now makes meals for Kwajo and his family just to say thank you. For his part, Kwajo is grateful to every person out there who has allowed him to share their story, because he knows that his campaign owes everything to their voices: 'That's why I constantly go back and thank them, because if it wasn't for them just sharing....' He tails off, knowing that it is those voices he is amplifying that are pushing any changes he can make. Just think how insignificant it must have made these people feel, to ask again and again for help with this basic human need, and to never be heard. He wants to show anybody who has been reduced to nothing but inconveniences to the very people who should be providing them with shelter 'that they do have a voice and they do matter'.

But Kwajo knows there are thousands and thousands more out there. If people in power are beginning to listen, he knows that this is a wake-up call that should have happened years ago. Needless to say, the shadow of the Grenfell disaster looms over everything that he does – if only people had been listening to the plight of social housing tenants back then, what might have been different? It's about priorities, and care. Does he feel our government takes the issues of housing seriously enough? As he says, 'I could go into Parliament and say to each one of them, "Would you live in these circumstances?" and I can guarantee that not one of them would say they would. So why do they think it's acceptable for the average person off an estate to?'

Kwajo's campaign has become his life – and the speed with which it has done so is extraordinary. Barely a year on from that first post and he is a spokesman raising awareness through every channel he can muster. In a matter of months, he had become the spokesman for a huge sector of society. The issue has changed not only his life but also his mindset – his ambitions aren't centred on the kinds of things you expect a 23-year-old to be thinking about – a flashy job, a nice car. He has become more and more aware that for him 'success' is bound up in the impact you have, in the ways you can make other people's lives better. He uses a phrase that I'm coming to hear more and more from the humble heroes I meet: that the sense of satisfaction he gets from helping people is 'something that money can't buy'. In fact, he has had people approach him with ideas about making money from what he is doing, but his response is clear: he never came into this for the money. For him, the reward lies in knowing he is making a real and lasting difference.

A better champion for the cause cannot be imagined: he is passionate and rightly furious on people's behalf, but he is also measured, articulate, impressive and unignorable. He is young, but he talks with the authority of someone who has lived through the problems he is describing. His drive is relentless, the good humour and determination with which he tackles this enormous problem is remarkable.

I chat to him over Zoom from the home where it all started –

the walls now properly plastered, the ceiling restored, the décor clean and minimalist, everything tidy – and as we talk, I feel an odd mixture of emotions: admiration, because Kwajo has to be one of the most impressive people I have met; gratitude, because I am glad that he has become the champion he has for those people out there who need him; but also fury, because it really shouldn't have to be this way. It shouldn't be up to a 23-year-old with a smartphone and a social media account to try and fix the slum conditions that people are having to live in. It should be down to the CEOs who are entrusted with the wellbeing of the people they house, and are well paid for their jobs. And they should be being held to account by the politicians who we put in place to guard our interests. Looking at Kwajo's Twitter feed, it's impossible not to feel that this is a simple moral equation that is out of balance. It's just not right.

One day, Kwajo wants to get back to the art that he's always wanted to do. Or perhaps something in the media. But there's no doubt he has caught the activism bug: also on his radar is the problem of rough sleeping and homelessness. He has half an eye on politics itself – perhaps the London mayoral elections in two years' might prompt him to try his luck. Frankly, I think he should aim for the top. You get the feeling Kwajo will achieve anything he sets out to do, and if one day we see him going for Downing Street, well, he'd get my vote.

Redemption Roasters

Inside one of the workshop units in HMP The Mount, a Category C men's prison in Hertfordshire, is a massive gleaming piece of equipment, all metal pipes and chrome engineering. It's a piece of kit that looks like it means business, which indeed it does: it's a central part of a particularly interesting social enterprise. Meanwhile, in ten different locations across the heart of London, busy cafés decked out in smart navy-blue paint are full of customers enjoying their morning espressos or lingering over afternoon cappuccinos. That piece of equipment is a state-of-the-art coffee roastery, those cafés are called Redemption Roasters, and they are both part of a speciality coffee company with a social conscience, which is helping a very under-served part of the population: ex-prisoners.

Here are some statistics: 46 per cent of ex-prisoners go on to reoffend within 12 months of their release – what is sometimes referred to as a 'revolving door' that keeps the prison population returning again and again. At the same time, unemployment among ex-prisoners runs five times higher than in the general population; only 36 per cent of prisoners go on to find work in the first two years after release. There are obviously many complex factors that lead to prisoners reoffending, but lack of meaningful employment is certainly one of them, and in fact prisoners that do find employment are 50 per cent less likely to reoffend. In other words, once you're in that system, it can be very hard to get out, and if we want people to stay out of prisons, one of the best ways to do that is also the hardest – help them find jobs.

This is exactly the problem that Redemption Roasters is here to address. At first it sounds like a bit of a strange juxtaposition: the toughness of the prison population set against the highfalutin world of posh coffee, with its latte art and discussions about tasting notes and the provenance of beans. But in practice, this is a genius innovation, providing prisoners with education, training and, where possible, employment. Not to mention the fact that the coffee is extremely good, which, in the end, is why the whole thing works.

The Redemption Roasters story started not long ago, in 2015, when Ted Rosner and Max Dubiel were looking to set up a business in the coffee industry. Their first aims had nothing to do either with prisons, or indeed with cafés themselves: they were intending to set up a coffee wholesaling business. Visiting a coffee industry fair to help germinate their ideas, they were approached by a representative from the Ministry of Justice, who put an unusual proposition to them: would they be interested in running barista courses in prisons? This was an intriguing idea, and it made sense: barista training is an instantly transferable skill which you can use anywhere, the basics can be taught in a relatively short amount of time (though many people would argue true mastery can take months if not years) and, most of all, it's a really good entry point into the hospitality industry.

Max and Ted looked into the barista idea, but when they came back to the MoJ, they had a counter proposition. Rather than just running barista courses, what if they also set up their roastery inside the prison too? This would allow for some paid employment for inmates, getting them involved in the roasting and production side, and this, combined with the barista training, would give them skills they could hope to use on their release.

And that is what happened: the first roastery was set up within HMP Aylesbury Young Offender Institution (demand later meant that it needed more space and transferred to HMP The Mount). Setting up a roastery in these circumstances wasn't straightforward, as you can imagine. There was a lot to negotiate: the logistics of setting up commercial-grade equipment inside a prison, working within the necessarily inflexible prison system, ensuring that the delivery of goods in and out of the prison ran smoothly. All of these were issues that Max and Ted probably hadn't contemplated when they first had the idea of setting up a coffee business. Alongside that, they also provided barista training courses in three other prisons that would last around six weeks. Most importantly, they did what they could through industry links to gain their graduates jobs on release. We're not talking about the odd phone call here – graduates from the courses who were interested in taking it further on release were given an employment support worker to help both them and their prospective employer, given access to career development and mental health workshops, and loans for laptop use and emergency funds. In other words, Redemption Roasters pledged to give the ex-offenders as much support in navigating the outside world as possible.

★

While the roastery and the barista academies proved a success, the really revolutionary moment for Redemption Roasters came a few years later, in 2018, when they took the step of setting up their own coffee shop in the heart of London. This was a huge shift, because it gave them a chance to prove their own point: to employ their own baristas themselves, 'making them part of the Redemption Roasters family on the outside' as Joe Tarbert, the education team leader, puts it.

Their first shop opened on Lamb's Conduit Street in Bloomsbury. This was pitching their tent in a really competitive environment: it's an upmarket shopping street that services everyone from office workers to the local population to NHS staff from Great Ormond Street Hospital opposite. And it was already home to some very good coffee outfits: definitely no shortage of choice for the discerning customer. Their café was going to have to be properly good if people were not just going to come, but keep coming back. The story behind Redemption Roasters is compelling, and it might get customers through the door, but the thing that will make loyal customers out of them is the quality of the product and the experience. The team knew their coffee was good – it was tried and tested in the market through the wholesale side of their business – but there wasn't any guarantee that the café would be a success. 'This wasn't about coffee nerds any more, this was about the average man on the street: are they going to engage with it?' says Joe. It must have been a bit of a nail-biting moment, waiting to see whether the concept and the place would pay off, but it did. Luckily for them, the coffee is very good, and the café, with its utilitarian but classy vibe, was a hit.

Four years later, in 2022, Redemption Roasters has ten coffee shops across London, and employs 14 of their graduates within those shops. Lockdowns of course proved a problem, but they soldiered on, selling takeaways instead of eating in. They have four training academies – in HMP Highdown, HMP Bullingdon and more recently in HMP Send (the first one they started in a woman's prison), and HMP Pentonville. On top of all of this, they have also opened a community-based academy. This was in part brought about by the pandemic, which naturally curtailed their operations within the prisons (although they were categorised as an essential operation so that the roastery could keep going, there were further restrictions on the inmates working there and in the training academies). The community academy – opened first in a shipping container in Hackney and later moving to King's Cross – is there to cater for people on the outside who might have been in prison in the past, or who the team feels may be at risk of ending up within the criminal justice system. 'It's a pretty broad definition,' says Joe, 'but people who have been homeless, who have issues with mental health, young people who are marginalised or otherwise are finding it hard to get into work.' The aim is that by coming to the community space, they will be given the basic skills of being a barista over five days. After that, the team supports them in finding jobs, either within Redemption Roasters or through connections in the hospitality industry.

One graduate of the community hub was a guy who presented himself to the Islington café. This was someone who had been homeless and in and out of prison, but having heard about Redemption Roasters he came to them and said, 'I'm really keen to learn, really keen to get involved, what can I do?' After five days' training in the community hub, he was employed by one of the cafés, and has now 'become totally immersed in it', revelling in everything from coffee snobbery to his own latte art. He dreams of one day having his own coffee shop. It's the kind of story that makes the Redemption Roasters concept so powerful.

★

I love the idea that these guys in this really tough environment are going on to become snobs about beans, caffeine content, the best roast and all that goes with posh coffee, but I'm curious as to how they tend to receive the concept at first. According to Joe, there can be a bit of a barrier initially, but 'once we get the guys behind the grinder, they kind of get hooked because it's something so different… Get them in a room with a coffee machine and a milk jug and suddenly they're obsessing about getting the perfect love heart on top of their latte. It becomes a real point of pride for them.'

I'm also intrigued about how the initiative tends to be received by the prison staff, who likely have seen more than one well-meaning project come and go over the years. What makes the programme work for both staff and inmates, says Joe, is that it is a skill that can translate to the outside. Frothy as latte art may seem (sorry about the pun), hospitality is an absolutely massive industry. 'We say to the guys, if you can be a barista in London, you can be a barista anywhere.' Redemption Roasters holds out the promise of a real outcome, something that inmates really want to make work: this tends to translate into a more positive attitude and, in turn, better behaviour. Of course there can be a level of cynicism among the prison staff about how well certain inmates will take to it all once they are released, so it must be a particularly satisfying moment for the team when they are able to go back and report on how well they are doing.

Of course, it would be naïve to think that everything is always easy with an enterprise like this. There are challenges at every level – even on the logistical one: it's not easy running a business knowing that a completely unrelated event in a prison could shut your production down (thankfully a reasonably rare event). Not to mention the challenges of employing people on their release, which is never going to be straightforward. No matter how much the education team do to support them, of course there are times when it doesn't work out, when a placement suddenly collapses out of the blue: 'We've supported guys for months at a time and it's all going swimmingly, and then suddenly they don't turn up for work, and you can't get hold of them, and then after making a day's worth of enquiries you find they've been breaching their licence and they're back inside.'

The business is set up in a way that can absorb this happening, but it is of course an emotional setback, one that the team has to be prepared for. And they know that beyond all the other challenges that lie on the outside for ex-prisoners, the work itself can be tough – working in a busy London coffee shop is not an easy gig, Joe says, 'and you're putting guys in there who come with all sorts of trauma and different experiences.' It's a juggling act, of course, trying to make sure that they are properly supported through all this and are doing the job well. The guys have to negotiate all sorts of situations that are not going to feel familiar to them, not least how to deal with customers, who are sometimes difficult or rude. One challenge has been to help the graduates deal with situations where they think customers have been disrespectful to themselves or their colleagues. Often coming from backgrounds where respect is a currency in itself, it can feel very unnatural for them to smile, let it wash over them and turn the other cheek.

It is also a situation where guys who have had at best a pretty mixed experience of authority figures – from policemen who they perceive as having been unfair, to prison staff who have been telling them what to do – have to learn to work with shop managers, who may well be a university graduate in their early twenties, and who is 'telling them you need to go wash those dishes, or that coffee's not quite good enough'. But this is all part of the point of the training, learning that the reality of working is sometimes doing stuff you don't want to.

I'm excited to be talking to Redemption Roasters not just because they're a great team with a great idea, but because as a social enterprise they represent a sector of our economy that I think is incredibly interesting, and which is growing year on year. The whole point is 'to marry profit and purpose'. That is, the social impact and the business depend on one another. 'We can have a great social impact because we have a great business. And we have a great business because we have a great social impact,' Joe says. For the whole thing to work, it has to be a viable and successful coffee company. They want to make coffee that sells; if it works, the business will thrive and they can keep training more baristas, offering more employment opportunities and helping more people.

There's something brilliantly interesting and compelling about a business like this, and it is a model we are seeing more and more of, with social enterprises springing up that cover everything from beer (Toast Ale), to loo paper (whogivesacrap. org) and even search engines (Ecosia). It's potentially such a great concept: imagine if we build ethical ideas into every single purchase we make. That's why the Redemption Roasters team are humble heroes to me: they may look like an average coffee shop on the outside – on the inside they are a team dedicated to making a real change. This doesn't come easy – you can tell talking to Joe how much work goes on behind the scenes by the education and support team, but it comes with its own rewards. It's fantastic hearing these stories from Joe, like the inmate from Aylesbury who started out working at the roastery there, and loved it to such an extent that he started to live, breathe and sleep coffee. On his release he worked first of all for the company itself, and then moved on to an independent specialist coffee outfit, where he has become head roaster. It's an extraordinary turnaround for someone who not that long ago was behind bars.

Or the guys who were graduates of the barista course in prison, who last month felt confident enough to join in with the latte art competition that the company runs every couple of months. (It's 'a coffee nerd's dream,' says Joe.) Thinking of these guys, who have gone from never having touched a coffee machine to standing in front of 60 people, ready to show off their skills, the whole place rooting for them and cheering their names, letting them know they are part of something, well... 'That for me is the success,' says Joe.

I find it very moving, this conjunction of this gourmet coffee world with these guys who have been through some really difficult journeys. As Joe says, 'It's very easy to feel as though there's no real hope on release. That as an ex-offender, you're always going to be labelled as an ex-offender, nobody's going to want to employ you.' In the end, I think, Redemption Roasters are selling more than one thing. Yes, they're in the business of coffee, but they are also in the business of hope.

Gabby Edlin

Some problems really shouldn't need a hero to fix them, but they do. In an ideal world, there wouldn't be people in this country who are struggling to fund necessities. But we don't live in that world, and at the time I write this, more and more people are in this position every day. One very basic need that any person who menstruates has, every single month, is for products to deal with their period. Unfortunately, as Gabby Edlin, founder and CEO of the organisation Bloody Good Period, knows, there are too many people out there for whom getting hold of these products is a recurring, undignified problem. For the last six years, she has been doing everything she can to change that.

One of the things I have really loved about writing this book is discovering where the very first seeds of the ideas for all the different projects came from. In Gabby's case, that moment came six years ago, in 2016, when she went to help out at an asylum drop-in centre at a synagogue she was connected to. As a Jewish person, the plight of refugees feels very immediate to her – her ancestors were refugees, and that is something, she says, that is 'in my DNA'. So she is perhaps more alert than most to the struggles that asylum seekers have to go through. This particular centre was a great resource – a once-a-month drop-in where asylum seekers could come and be helped out with the essentials: they were given clothes, food, nappies, legal advice – all the basics. It happened that Gabby had recently read an article by the journalist Maya Oppenheim, who asked a question which hadn't occurred to Gabby before: 'What do homeless women do on their periods?' The answer was, 'Well, it's incredibly hard.' That question, and the lack of a proper answer, had stayed with her. So when she joined the discussion with the group of volunteers about how to organise the supplies, Gabby was primed to notice one particular void in the provisions they were handing out. What did they do about period products – where were the pads and tampons and pantyliners? And the entirely well-meaning answer was that they didn't have a regular stock: these were things that could be supplied, if asked for, 'in an emergency'.

Gabby's immediate realisation was that a period should never be an emergency. It is a very, very predictable occurrence: if you are someone who menstruates, it is going to happen roughly once a month. It should just be part of life. But if you don't have products to deal with it, an emergency is what it's going to turn into. As we've already seen with Jem Stein and The Bike Project, asylum seekers in particular have extremely limited resources: as I write, they get £40.85 per week, and they are not allowed to work. That £40.85 has to cover food, transport, clothes, medicines – all the essentials of life.

Period products – that regular and unavoidable necessity – are highly expensive relative to that. Just to put that expense into perspective, Bloody Good Period calculates an average cost of a period as £10 per month (£4 on tampons, £4 on pads, £2 on panty liners) – a conservative estimate. Multiply that up over 40 years, and that's nearly £5,000 over a lifetime; a huge amount. Or to put it another way, if you are existing on £39 per week, that is one-sixteenth of your entire monthly income, just to deal with something nature throws at you every single month. Someone with heavy periods might need to spend a whole lot more.

This problem is no doubt made a lot worse by the fact that periods have, throughout the world and throughout history, been 'surrounded by shame and silence and stigma and taboo', as Gabby so eloquently puts it. If someone is in the direst of circumstances – is a refugee or an asylum seeker or is homeless – the last thing they want to do is to have to make a fuss about this very basic need.

Seeing the issue laid out so clearly in front of her, Gabby just could not ignore it. So she went on Facebook (that was the medium back then) and asked people to donate. The seed that would become Bloody Good period was sown.

Pretty quickly, it became clear that there was one crucial aspect to the project: by its very nature this could not be an ad-hoc service, available when the products happened to be there. It was only ever going to work if the supply was consistent, sustainable and constant. In other words, women turning up at the drop-ins had to know that the products were going to be reliably available. As Gabby puts it, 'With people who have been so rejected by society and made to feel they have committed a crime just by seeking safety, trust cannot be built easily. So you can't just turn up with a couple of packs of tampons once in a while.'

Having first identified this as an issue for asylum seekers, Gabby soon realised that it went far further than that. There were too many people in society for whom this extra expense once a month was unmeetable. She wanted to reach anybody experiencing period poverty, so as well as asylum drop-in centres, she aimed at getting period products into food banks, homeless charities, and other organisations providing for those in need. That may sound like an easy enough proposition, but if you think about it, it was far from simple: how do you ensure a steady supply of good-quality, in-date products to all these different places? At first, Bloody Good Period would get donations of physical products, which would be sorted, stored and then delivered to the various partnerships she was working with by volunteers. The pandemic changed this model – now they ask for online donations of money with which they can place bulk orders from suppliers who deliver direct to the centres. In fact, there are advantages to working this way, not least that it means they are never dealing with products that might be out of date or damaged.

In all, by the middle of 2022, Bloody Good Period had given out more than 218,000 packs of period products – including reusables. That's a hell of a lot of people helped, a lot of dignity saved. They also run education programmes for refugee women, having learned through the process of giving out products that there was sometimes a lack of education around this, and certainly that these women were typically accessing healthcare very rarely. They offer consultations and sessions with healthcare professionals – nurses and gynaecologists – about 'anything in the underwear' as Gabby puts it – everything from breast and cervical cancer to the menopause.

★

As well as all of this, Bloody Good Period does everything they can to normalise the subject of menstruation. Gabby fought an interesting battle for the very name of the organisation – the Charity Commission was horrified at the idea of registering a name that combined the words 'bloody' and 'period'. The words on their own were fine, but 'they didn't like the idea of bloody and period together.' It took a while for Gabby to convince them that the name was the whole point: it had to bring people up a bit short, make them laugh, make them notice. The Bloody Good Period website is a masterpiece of straight-talking good sense, couched in language that is funny, direct and real. 'I suppose I always thought that if it makes people uncomfortable, that is not the same as the feeling of not having period products, and having to live with the anxiety and the stress, and the potential physical difficulties such as infections. They're not the same thing, so I'm not going to give them equal weight,' says Gabby.

The conversation about periods has moved on in recent years – we're at least a bit further on from when pads were advertised using only blue liquids just in case somebody might – shock horror – associate red liquid with blood. I've noticed recently that female athletes, from footballers to swimmers, will talk much more openly about training for their menstrual cycle.

It was only 2015 when tennis player Heather Watson caused actual headlines for mentioning in an interview that her exit from the Australian Open happened during her period, and I'm glad to say things do seem to have progressed a little since then. But there is still a reticence to talk about periods openly – it still feels transgressive somehow. Gabby wants to get to a point where we can just feel comfortable having those conversations – if we can't, then there are all sorts of conditions, from really bad periods to endometriosis, which are going to be hidden and stigmatised. She is running an employer's programme to increase openness about periods in the workplace, working with some big companies to raise awareness of the issue.

Ideally, Bloody Good Period simply wouldn't need to exist. The Scottish government, for example, has recently undertaken to provide free period products to anybody in need of them. Bloody Good Period helps people to lobby their MPs to follow Scotland's example. Until that happens, it is there to ensure that everyone has what they need – from appropriate products to proper conversations – to make sure their periods go as smoothly as possible.

★

There's a brilliantly practical ambition to Gabby's approach – she sees an issue, she founds a whole organisation to deal with it – but I don't think that practicality should mask what has clearly been an incredible amount of work. She has taken Bloody Good Period from a realisation that there was a need to a fully fledged organisation, one that is helping thousands and thousands of people.

As it happens, I talk to Gabby just a few days before she

hands over the reins of the charity to one of her team. It's clearly going to be a wrench to move on – she is aiming to work with a range of charities to help them get their messages across, and she's obviously going to be amazing at that. But what she has achieved is incredible. She is clearly – and rightly – really proud of the work she has done, but there is definitely something in her that baulks at the idea of being called any kind of hero.

Most of all, she is really keen not to feel that what she has done has changed anybody's life, because that isn't the way it should be – lives shouldn't be transformed just by a pack of sanitary pads. Success, for her, is simply a woman who on her visit to a drop-in centre picks up period products for herself and perhaps her daughter and her neighbour, without even giving it a second thought. And, more widely, success would be a society where nobody feels embarrassed or ashamed to talk about a normal bodily function, or has to feel humiliated to get hold of the products they need to deal with it. She would, she says, be horrified by the idea of extravagant thanks, because nobody should be in the position of having to thank anyone for something so basic. 'When we've done our job well, people don't think about us, which is really great and the way we want it to be.'

Well, she's right in one way, of course. But I also think that what she does is deserving of thanks and recognition, not from individual women, but from society in general. She's changing the conversation, ensuring that everyone has access to the period products they need, and looking out for the needs of others. For that, even if she would prefer me not to, I'm glad to call her a hero.

Hussain Manawer

My next humble hero is a young man from Ilford in East London. This is someone who has shared stages with everyone from Ed Sheeran to Meghan Markle. Who has performed his poetry with Tyson Fury. Who has been commissioned to write poems by everyone from the Mayor of London to the BBC. Who was featured in Oprah Winfrey and Prince Harry's seminal documentary series *The Me You Can't See*. Whose first book of poetry has just been launched and has already become a *Sunday Times* bestseller. Who at the age of only 31 has gained more accolades than I can even list. To which you might say, 'With a profile like that, is he still a humble hero?' And I would answer: 'Absolutely.'

There are two reasons why Hussain Manawer, wherever his career takes him, is always going to be one of my humble heroes. The first is just that that is who he is as a person. I've known him for seven years now, and he is still the same fantastically warm and normal spirit at heart – an East End boy who loves his mum. And second, because all of the work he does, all the poems he writes, all the performances he gives, are in the service of a truly important cause: to help prove that mental health matters, and that the more we talk about it and raise awareness, the better.

★

I first met Hussain back in 2015 when he had just been given the One Young World's Kruger Cowne Rising Star award. This was a year-long quest by this prestigious youth summit to find someone they would dub 'The Voice of a Generation', and who would win a trip to space. Yes, seriously, that was the actual prize: to go into space. After a gruelling process, Hussain had made it down to the final three, each of whom would have to perform a three-minute keynote speech onstage at the One Young World summit in Bangkok, in front of an audience that included luminaries such as Kofi Annan and Bob Geldof. On the night, Hussain, looking nervous but determined in a tweed jacket, had absolutely stormed it with his poem 'My Name is Hussain'. It was a barnstorming performance that was an honest rendering of everything that mattered to him. Funny and angry and heartfelt, it laid bare his mental health struggles and gave a blistering take on the state of the world. There was no doubting his ability to move mountains with the power of his words. The audience were applauding practically from the first line, rose to their feet at the end, and Hussain won the award.

I remember speaking to him the next morning – he was still clearly dazed and dazzled by the whole event – and just laughing at the incongruousness of it, because there was this young man who had won this extraordinary accolade. But he was also just a boy from down the road in London whose dad had a restaurant and whose mum was terrified that he might leave home. And now he had won an award that had named him spokesman for his generation, and was planning to send him off to do astronaut training. Not only that, but he hadn't even told his mum what the prize was; he was too scared of her reaction. There was just something about his spirit which caught me: such an open and honest person, willing to talk about the difficult things but always with an energy and a desire to connect. He was just a fountain of words and ideas, and he was just determined to do whatever he could to open up the conversation about mental health.

So where did all this wisdom and brilliance with words stem from, in a boy whose household growing up was not big on literature? ('The only book I had in my house to read was the Argos catalogue, and I would be flicking through that religiously.') The spark was lit a long time ago: he started writing poetry at the age of 13 while still at school. The urge to perform had perhaps come a few years earlier, when his primary school choir had sung at the Royal Albert Hall. 'That was my first insight into the world of entertainment, big red curtains and all, and I absolutely loved it,' he says now. But the poetry itself came later, first of all in the form of rap lyrics that he kept hidden, jotted in the back of his school planner. The catalyst came just after he had been in a bit of trouble at school and got suspended: a new teacher, who didn't know him, came across his poems and entered him into a poetry slam competition. This was his first time ever performing by himself onstage, and he did a piece about identity. It was then that 'something was lit inside me,' he says.

Still, no matter how drawn he was to poetry, he was still a teenage boy and poetry might not always be the coolest thing in the world at that age. On the one hand, he couldn't get enough of it – he remembers studying a Carol Ann Duffy poem at school: 'I deciphered this thing like it was code, man.' On the other, when he told the people around him that he was writing his own poetry, the reaction was generally laughter. It didn't help that he came from a background where it didn't come naturally to people to talk so openly about their emotions, and emotions were what his poetry was all about: cutting through to the honesty of how he was really feeling.

So for a long while he kept his work hidden, but nothing stopped him 'writing, always writing, writing, writing'. As he grew older and went to university, he grew bolder, and started entering open-mic nights, performing anywhere he could. (In his wildest dreams he would probably have loved to go to a performing arts school, rather than studying quantity surveying, but his mother wouldn't countenance that.)

At all the various jobs he was doing at this time – everything from working at Currys PC World to Primark to Sainsbury's, to being an usher at the O2 arena or Shakespeare's Globe, he found he was soaking up everything, looking out for the tiny details that would find their way into his words, his mind going at a million miles a minute. It was this path that was eventually to lead to the One Young World conference that would change his life.

I just absolutely love Hussain's description of his preparation for that summit. Once he'd entered the competition and got to the finalist stage, he worked up his piece, and the night before he was due to fly out to Bangkok, he performed it for his friends in Nando's car park in Beckton. He played the instrumental music out of the speakers of his car and gave his performance.

'You're going to win this,' they said.

'Why do you say that?' asked Hussain.

'Because it's just so raw, so just don't lose that essence when you get there.'

So there was Hussain, flying alone across the world, thinking about their words in that car park and convincing himself to keep focused: 'You've flown however many hours across the world to speak for three minutes. Better make those three minutes count.'

He certainly did that, and he's been making it count ever since.

★

Now this was at a point when people were not talking about mental health in the way that they do now. The conversation was just beginning to start, but by no means had it hit the mainstream: it just wasn't something that was on the agenda yet for most high-profile companies and organisations. And Hussain did not come from the kind of background where this was a natural thing to talk about. Men in particular were not encouraged to talk about uncomfortable emotions, let alone make them public on a world stage. So for Hussain to do that, and even more, to do it through poetry, which is not an easy art form, was a real step into the unknown. His work takes him to the darkest of subjects – his poems might address addiction, suicide, depression – but always with a warmth and a heart that rooted them in the real world, and an optimistic, hopeful message: if we can be real, if we can talk about these things, the door is always open for things to improve.

The higher the profile Hussain got, the more he found he could help people. In the early days, if he didn't get the response he wanted, that just prompted him to do more and work harder. It didn't mean he didn't feel the knockbacks he sometimes got. He found it as scary as the next person to bound onto a stage and talk about his innermost feelings, and yet he continued to do it. Why? I think he just felt like that was his job: 'The biggest blessing of being a poet is to be able to receive people's emotions for a living,' he says. That's quite a statement, when you think about it – the privilege and responsibility of talking right to the heart of what matters to people. 'I think if I can help people relate to something, whether privately or publicly, my work is done, because there's comfort in relating to people and that's something I hope my work does.'

I think this is what makes Hussain's poems so magical. He seems to have the ability to talk to every listener and make them believe he is talking just to them. I mean, I'm a 47-year-old father of two, and they resonate with me just as they do with a much younger generation. I've introduced him on stage before, and the whole place just had this amazing energy, people jumping around and cheering. There's a huge enthusiasm, combined with an honesty and rawness, to his work that I think allows people to open up to what he is saying to them, and reflect it back into their own lives.

★

Ever since that first interview in 2015 I've kept in touch with Hussain, and I watched over the next couple of years as he went from strength to strength. Having achieved a platform with his life-changing One Young World success, it was typical of him that he immediately started to use that platform by attempting to put together a Guinness World Record attempt for the largest mental health lesson ever held – something he achieved in 2017 when he and psychologist Professor Dame Til Wykes gave a presentation for 538 schoolchildren from 14 schools at the Hackney Empire.

He returned to the One Young World conference a year after his victory – this time in Ottawa – and delivered an extraordinarily moving poem called 'Mother Tongue' – a call to arms for anyone who was trying to fight their demons on their own. It's such a raw and honest poem, guaranteed to speak to anybody who has had their own long, dark nights and who has tried to hide their pain from their loved ones.

The strongest theme that his poetry returned to again and again was his mother, and the role that she played in his life. She was absolutely the guiding light in his world, and all his poems – but perhaps 'Mother Tongue' in particular, which dealt with his admission to her of the internal struggles he had been going through – returned always to her. She was just the source of everything for him: his humour, his sense of home, his determination to do well for her. Whenever I heard him speak, he would bring her to life through the tiniest of details – I could picture her as a force of nature, ruling her house and her kitchen, admonishing him always for getting food on his clothes when he ate, laughing and joking and coming up with the world's best advice.

To the world, he was becoming a mental health campaigner who could fill auditoriums just with the power of poetry. To her, he was just her little boy who needed to be looked after. When he finally got round to telling her about the potential trip to space, she told him not to go. When he asked why, she said, 'Because if anything happened to you up there, then I wouldn't be able to come and help you.' Whatever heights he reached, he was always a mother's boy at heart.

Which is why his heart was ripped out of him when, in 2017, his mother died, very suddenly, of a brain aneurysm. This young man who had already been struggling with his mental health had been dealt the one of the worst blows life could throw at him. He had started out by talking about mental health and drawing on his own experiences of how hard depression could be, but from this point on grief was going to be in the DNA of what he did. It was a cruel lesson in the truth that, as he puts it now, 'Pain, heartbreak and loss do not discriminate, they will find you, whoever you are in this world.'

In the wake of her death he was absolutely stricken, to the point where he was barely functioning, and it took one of his best friends to give him the advice that he needed: 'You need to write your way out of it.' Writing became the only way he could deal with his emotions, using his own words as a guide to get him through. He feels now that the many, many poems he wrote at that time – trying simply to write himself through the pain – were almost a gift from his mum, because as he says, 'I look at every emotion you get as a gift, be it pain, love, sadness, whatever.' As he so beautifully puts it, 'If you felt loved you will eventually feel pain, and if you feel pain it is because you were loved. We have to understand there is no bargaining here: you can't have one without the other.'

In one of those twists of fate, the same week that Hussain's mother died, he discovered that the planned trip to space that he had been anticipating and working towards was not going to happen. At any time, this would have been a cruel blow, but compared to his mother's death, it didn't seem to matter. After all, she had not wanted him up there anyway...

The next years would be spent trying to get through his loss, which would blindside him at the most unexpected of times. But being the man he is, that pain and grief was gradually transformed into poems that would provide a comfort to other people suffering their own losses. Those poems, those gifts his mother had given him, turned out to be gifts that he passed on to the world. If what we need most in times of bereavement is connection, the feeling that other people understand what you are going through, then those poems do exactly that. They lay bare the way grief can assault you through the tiniest of moments; they describe how it can undermine all the other successes in your life, but eventually, though they are full of heartbreak, they are full of his mother's spirit and laughter too. In the end, you can feel how his mother remains a comforting presence to him – his poems are in some ways still a conversation with her. In the poems, she stands at his side; he speaks to her, and she speaks back. Hussain always remembers something his mum would say to him – if she were to die, she said, she wanted him and his siblings to, as she would put it, 'cry and get over it'. It has been a line that has revolved in his head. You have to cry; you have to acknowledge your grief. But you also have to move on. It was a hard-won piece of knowledge for his mum, whose own mother had died when she was young, but it was typical of the relationship between Hussain and his mother that she had given him the very tools he needed to get over her. 'Those words were a lifeline... you need to cry, you need to cry a lot, and you need to get over it.' When people in the wake of her death would say to him, 'What would your mum say if she was here?' he already knew the answer: she had given it to him.

That is why he is so passionate about the need for families to have the real conversations, the hard conversations, while they still can. 'It starts at home, because the day you're no longer here, you're no longer here... You need to guide them as much as you can': Those words of hers saved him, he believes.

The very sad irony in all this is that Hussain's mother never saw him perform. Something had always held her back from attending his open-mic nights or other performances, and it was only when he was coming up to his first headline show in London that she bought a dress to come and see him. 'But she passed away before the show,' says Hussain, leaving him bereft. 'I tell myself she was never meant to see it, she was just meant to see me as her son, in the house, happy, smiling, spilling food on my clothes. She was just meant to see that. She wasn't meant to see anything else. I don't think she would have understood it.'

★

It won't have escaped your notice that the conversation about mental health has changed a lot in the last five years or so. And Hussain has been at the forefront of this, always doing what he can to keep the conversation going. He became an ambassador for the Samaritans, putting out an EP called 'Am I going too deep?' in support of them, and helped to launch their Big Listen campaign. He used his online profile – Hussain's House – to raise awareness and launch a mental health youth festival. Wherever he could, he was using the power of his words to change the conversation. In early 2020 he wrote and performed an amazing poem about loneliness, for the GMB 1 Million Minutes campaign, and has been involved with it ever since: his exceptionally moving 'Dear Britain', for the second campaign during lockdown was an extraordinary summing up of everything the country had faced during that terrible year.

In 2021 his script was used for the Royal Mental Health minute – a co-ordinated campaign by the Duke and Duchess of Cambridge's Heads Together charity – in which his script about mental health was read out simultaneously across every radio station in the country, by a cast of celebrities that ranged from David Beckham to Joanna Lumley to the Cambridges themselves. (Hussain tells me that when he got the call saying that his work had been chosen for this honour, he was in the bed shop Dreams in Beckton, mattress shopping. 'Wow', he thought, 'maybe I deserve a better mattress!')

And, of course, there was the call from Oprah Winfrey's people one day, not only wanting to feature him in *The Me You Can't See* documentary, but wanting to use one of his poems on the trailer. At first, he was slightly panicked, thinking he was about to have the worst case of writer's block ever, but then it turned out that they already had a poem in mind. Going right back to the beginning, they wanted to use 'My Name is Hussain' from the One Young World conference all those years ago. He couldn't help but laugh: the poem he had debuted in

Nando's car park, up there on a worldwide stage, next to Lady Gaga and Prince Harry.

He continues to tread a line – he is happy about how far the mental health conversation has come, but he knows how much further there is to go, particularly in certain communities – not just across ethnicities, but across socioeconomic groups too. Which is one reason why he tries hard in his work to have an arsenal of poems that will appeal to every different sort of audience. The currency of his job is empathy, and he works hard to understand as many different perspectives as possible: 'So if I'm in a prison in Elmley, or if I'm in Ilford library, or if I'm in a private school in Hertfordshire, I'll have something in my poetry palette that will be relatable.' It's all about connection. Hussain is wonderfully protective about his poems and where they end up. Sometimes he will write a poem and put it aside for a while, even sit on it for years while he waits for the right outlet. This happened with the poem 'You Are Not My Best Friend', which he wrote about addiction. He was proud of it, but he didn't know where it should go, until one day Tyson Fury's people called him and asked him for an example of his work. That became an incredibly powerful joint performance between the two of them: the poem had found its proper home.

Let me tell you one final story about Hussain that for me completely sums up what makes this lovely superhero truly humble. Not long ago he kindly asked if I would do an event with him for his book launch. This is the book that he had waited ten years to get published; waited until he knew that the time and the publisher were right. When he was younger, writing poems on his phone on the Central line on the way to work, he had dreamed of this moment, but it had taken him until 2022 before he found a publisher who he felt would treat him and his poems in the right kind of way. Finally, his first book, *Life is Sad and Beautiful*, was ready to be published. (As an aside, I love the way he dubs himself, right there on the cover, as 'The Original Mummy's Boy'.) This night had been a long time coming.

Having known Hussain as long as I have, I was very excited to see the book out there, and very honoured that he asked me to be a part of its publication. So there we are, just before the launch in a grand venue next to the Waterstones on Piccadilly, and I ask him, 'Right, how exactly do you want to do this?'

'Well, I'm going to invite this woman up to speak,' he says.

'OK,' I say, not quite understanding. 'Who's that then?'

It turned out to be a lovely woman he had connected with over social media, who has a son who is autistic and who is campaigning for a greater understanding of the condition. Hussain had suggested that she come to his book launch and use it as an opportunity to give a talk about her story and the issue of autism. I had to laugh: it was just so typical of Hussain. Here he was with this event that was absolutely all about him, an event that had taken ten years of work and poems and laying his soul bare to get to, and his first thought was, 'Let's get somebody else to share the platform.'

When I asked him why, he said there were two reasons for wanting her to do it. The first was just that he knew how hard it was to get a message across. Here she was with an issue she was incredibly passionate about, and here he was with a ready-made, captive audience. For him, it was just right that he share his stage. And secondly, she was a mum looking out for her son, and for Hussain there can be no more powerful relationship than that. So the woman made her speech, a really moving one about how neurodiversity is all around us and we need to be more alive to it and more accepting. And then of course Hussain talked about his own book, and it was a wonderful night and everyone was blown away by him, as they always are.

I thought, 'Wow, that was a moment that just summed him up.' Because no matter how many grand names are in his contacts list, or what extraordinary opportunities he has created for himself out of nothing but his own vulnerability, passion and talent, this is still a guy who believes most of all that the message should get out there; that people should hear about the mental health, or neurodiversity, or the truth of who we all are. And who cares enough to make sure that somebody else feels heard, on this night of all nights.

I know Hussain is going to be in my life for a very long time. I don't know where his talents and passion will lead him – I expect there will be many amazing twists and turns along the way. But I feel pretty confident that he will always remain the original mother's boy that he is, carrying his mum's legacy and his own fantastic honest and humble spirit wherever he goes.

Errol McKellar

For Errol McKellar, it all started because he was snoring. One day in 2010, he woke up to find his wife standing over him, telling him it was time he sorted it out. (In many ways, as you'll see, while Errol is definitely a humble hero, Sharon is also a heroine in this story.) It was Sharon who made him the appointment to see the doctor and Errol duly went along to see what they could do. As he sat in the waiting room, he happened to pick up a leaflet saying that men should get checked for prostate cancer. It wasn't something he had ever thought about before, but he decided to take the advice, went up to the receptionist to ask for an appointment to get tested, and was surprised to hear that as it was a simple blood test, they could do it on the spot. In Errol's case, that first blood test was followed by a second one, and then a biopsy, and a couple of weeks later he was back at the doctor's after a follow-up scan, to hear words that he was in no way prepared to hear: he had extensive cancer of the prostate.

I think Errol's reaction will resonate with anybody who has been given similar news: 'I just got up and walked out of the room and I went out of the building, sat in my car, and I think the word cancer hit me. And I'm not ashamed to tell you, as a man I cried like a baby. I don't know if I've ever experienced fear like that. I just felt lost and completely out of control about what I was going to do next.' Once again, it was Sharon who came to his rescue. She said to him, 'In all the years I've known you, I've never seen you quit on anything you've ever done.' He took her words as motivation through the ordeal that was to follow, starting with the moment when he wiped the tears from his eyes and went back into the doctor's surgery to talk about the operation that would be necessary.

Errol was both lucky and unlucky – unlucky in that the cancer had already spread beyond the perimeter walls, meaning that after the operation to remove it he would also need three months of radiotherapy, but lucky in that that leaflet meant they had caught it in time. There would be side effects, but that blood test, taken on a whim, had saved his life.

Here are some facts about prostate cancer: it is currently the biggest killer of men in this country. At the time I write, more than 47,000 men are diagnosed with it every year. Over 11,000 men a year die of it. One in 12 Asian men will have it in their lifetime. One in eight white men will have it, and one in four Afro-Caribbean men. Many people don't show any symptoms in the early stages. And the most important fact of all? If it is detected early enough, it is treatable – it's all about how soon you discover it. That is why getting tested is of utmost importance.

For the six months that Errol was off work for his radio-therapy and recuperation, all these facts were going round in his head. He wanted to do something meaningful with what had happened to him, but he couldn't see what that should be. He discussed it with Sharon, and again she came up with a line that was to motivate him: 'Listen,' she said, 'this cancer's only knocked you down, you know, it hasn't knocked you out. And you're going to go 12 rounds with it, but you'll take everyone with you.'

'OK', thought Errol. 'I'll go with that.'

At the time, Errol was a mechanic at a garage in Hoxton, east London. (Before that, he had been a youth coach at his beloved Leyton Orient for many years – football absolutely runs in his blood.) It was what happened on Errol's first day back at work that was to set him on the course that was to change not only his life, but a lot of other people's too. On that first morning, as Errol was getting used to the strangeness of being back at work, a customer came in to have his car serviced. He had heard about Errol's illness, and asked how he was doing. As the conversation progressed, Errol looked at him: 'And you know what, to this day I don't know why I said it: I asked, "When was the last time you had your prostate checked?"'

That brought the conversation down to earth with a bump, Errol recalls. 'What the hell has that got to do with my car's gearbox?' was the reply.

And without knowing where the idea came from, Errol said to him, 'OK, I tell you what, I'll give you a 20 per cent discount on the work I'm going to do on your car if you go and get your prostate checked by the time you come to pick it up.'

A few days later, the man returned, brandishing a bit of

paper in his hand. 'Oh Lord', went Errol's first thought. 'This has just cost me 200 quid.'

'Never mind the money, don't worry about that,' said the customer, 'but you'd better read this.' The letter he was holding said that he had 25 per cent cancer in his prostate. Luckily, they had caught it in time. That conversation with Errol had saved his life.

From then on, Errol dedicated himself to raising awareness of the condition. Every man that came in, he would talk to about it. Every woman, he would encourage to talk to their partners. He offered discounts to men who got tested, and he made sure that the conversation continued. In all, 48 of the thousands of men who took up his challenge to get tested were diagnosed with the condition. Two have very sadly passed away, but just think of it: over 40 lives saved. That is a pretty profound outcome from a simple car service.

I love the fact that a whole brilliant campaign was born from that first flash of inspiration on that first day back at work. Errol's straightforward but genius idea was this: 'MOT Yourself'. As far as he is concerned, it's all about talking. He knows as well as anyone that men don't like to talk about their health problems, let alone problems to do with the genital area. It's a mental health thing, for him: this is something that men struggle to confront, which means that talking about it needs to be normalised. So, as he says, just as you take your car in for its MOT every year, so you should be doing an annual MOT on everything to do with your own health. As he puts it, 'Would you drive your car with no brakes? The answer's no. So why walk down the road with the risk of cancer? You get yourself tested, and hopefully everything will be fine. But if not, then there is huge support out there and the cancer is curable if caught early.'

I know myself how common this cancer can be. My own dad got it, about 20 years ago when he was in his early fifties. I happened to go out to the pub with four schoolfriends at around that time, and told them the news. And of the four other people at that table, two of the others said, 'That's weird, so has mine.' That was three out of the five of us sitting round that table, whose dads were all roughly the same age. They all got treated in slightly different ways, and I'm delighted to say they are all still with us. But it was a powerful moment for us – that sudden understanding of how common it can be. Errol believes it is that kind of conversation that can change lives.

In pursuit of making sure those conversations happen, Errol turned his original idea into a charity, The Errol McKellar Foundation. As well as the MOT Yourself initiative, which has been rolled out to ten other garages, it also hosts weekly 'Sit & Talks' for men to open up and talk about health issues, and takes part in regular 'Walk & Talks'. He is particularly keen that men with an Afro-Caribbean heritage get themselves tested, and that they go further and take part in the research around why it is so prevalent in their community. He's optimistic for the future, believing that the pandemic has showed us all we have to take control of our own health.

So many of the humble heroes I have met for this book absolutely radiate joy and life, and Errol is definitely one of these. He's a man on a mission, and he goes about that mission with a huge smile on his face and warmth in his heart. I'm not at all surprised that he has become extremely beloved in his community, being nominated as an Olympic torchbearer in

2012, and receiving a Points of Light award, which recognises outstanding individual volunteers, from the government in 2016. In 2020 he was given a richly deserved MBE. It's pretty clear though that for all the recognition he has been given, the most important thing to him is the lives he has changed. How amazing must that realisation be, when somebody is treated successfully all due to a conversation that Errol initiated? 'That is the greatest satisfaction,' he says, 'because one of the things myself and Sharon say is that we don't want people to go through what we had to go through every day.'

Errol has now left the garage, but nothing is slowing him down. His main challenge for the future? The Errol McKellar Foundation has come up with yet another brilliant idea that he hopes to get on the road soon – a mobile testing unit. Knowing how little men like to go and see doctors, let alone go to hospitals, Errol wants to bring the testing to them. I can just see this at football grounds and events – a quick test while you wait for the match to start. How many lives could that save, in the same kind of time it takes to get a pint from the bar?

It's a great experience, talking to Errol. This is someone who has taken the worst thing that has happened in their own life, and done everything they can to save others from going through the same thing. Everything he says makes such good sense – apart from when he's trying to persuade me back onto the football pitch, that is – and a salient reminder to us all that we should keep an eye on our health. But in all of our conversations, there is one thing he says that sticks with me, because it's something that is true not only of his own amazing campaign but of so much of the work that all of these humble heroes do.

When I congratulate him on the difference he has made to so many lives, not just the men diagnosed through his own garage, but the thousands beyond that who have seen and listened to his campaign over the last 12 years, he is grateful but self-deprecating: 'It's not me who is going to make this change,' he says. 'It's we. All of us coming together and finding an inspiration.' For someone who has made as much of a difference as Errol, that is a pretty fantastic way to look at it.

And in case you were wondering, Errol did manage to sort his snoring out, much to Sharon's relief. Yes, he has to wear a contraption at night that makes him look like Darth Vader, but that's a price Sharon is certainly willing to make him pay!

trailblazing
heroes

Josh Llewellyn-Jones

When I hear the word superhuman, the image that comes into my mind is of a smiling Welshman, 35 years old, ridiculously muscled and good-looking, and more often than not undertaking some crazily extreme physical challenge. I picture him proudly trailing the Welsh flag as he runs into Cardiff's Principality Stadium for the triumphant last leg of an extreme triathlon challenge; or as a young guy of only 17 having a sparring match with a champion boxer on the top of Mount Kilimanjaro; or lifting weight after weight for 24 hours straight to smash yet another record.

But I also think of how, every single morning, he has to count out cupfuls of pills and down them – over 60 tablets in different shapes and sizes. That's because Josh Llewellyn-Jones is not just one of the fittest, most determined and most impressive athletes I know. He is also someone who lives – as he always has and always will – with cystic fibrosis.

The physical feats that Josh has undertaken are something

else: he holds world records that defy belief and are unmatched by anyone. But that's not the reason I call him one of my humble heroes: to me, what is most heroic about him is the inspiration he gives to other people, and especially children, who are also living with CF.

★

The first sign that anything was wrong with Josh's health came very early indeed: on the day he was born. It's a day his parents are unlikely to forget. He was born with a distended bowel that made his stomach so swollen that the skin was transparent. He was immediately rushed into surgery to remove a blockage. When this tiny baby emerged from that surgery, scarred and stitched up and with a colostomy bag and an abscess in his stomach that could not be removed, the doctors told his parents that he had a 10 per cent chance of surviving the night. Miraculously, Josh came through, after a long stint in intensive care, but the tests that were done revealed very quickly that he had cystic fibrosis. Not only that, but he had what is called the double delta F508 variant, the most common variant of the disease but also the worst. It was unlikely he would reach the age of 30, said the doctors.

It's impossible to overestimate the hammer blow this must have been to Josh's parents. Cystic fibrosis is a condition that, as he puts it, 'in a nutshell affects the lungs and the digestive system and all other vital organs and clogs them up with a thick sticky mucus.' His parents had to have a crash course in the realities of the condition: for the rest of his life, Josh would have to take enzymes every day simply to digest his food; the enzymes most of us produce automatically but which his pancreas doesn't create. He would often be on other pills too – vitamins, supplements, and antibiotics for the lung infections that CF sufferers are prone to and which are so dangerous to them. He would have to do physiotherapy every morning and every evening of his childhood, to prevent his lungs filling up with mucus. That physiotherapy wasn't going to be a gentle rub-down, either: 'My brothers would love it because they would essentially get to smack me on the chest without getting told off for 20 minutes at a time. And when I say smack, I mean really smack. It's pretty brutal, but it needs to be done to vibrate the mucus in the lungs to get it to shift,' Josh says now. And while most people think of CF as a condition of the lungs, in reality it affects all parts of the body, from the liver to the density of your bones.

Back in 1987, the life expectancy for a child with CF was frighteningly low – reaching the teenage years was expected, 30 was considered the outside margin. The advice at the time to parents of CF children was to take as much care of their children as possible – to avoid any danger of lung infections or over-exertion that might take a further toll on their already overloaded bodies. Effectively, to wrap them in cotton wool.

The thing was, that kind of parenting wasn't really Josh's dad's style. Adrian Llewellyn-Jones resolved to find out everything he could about how to manage the condition – quite a difficult call-back when there wasn't the internet and he had to rely on local libraries for information. When Josh was two, Adrian came across a doctor in Dallas, Texas, called Dr Bob Kramer, who was renowned for his advanced research and treatment for kids with CF. He took the whole family out to Dallas, and Josh spent a day undergoing every single test possible. At the end of the day Bob Kramer walked in with his entourage: 'Yes, it's definitely CF, and it's definitely the worst kind.'

'So what do we do?' asked Josh's parents.

Dr Kramer's answer was immediate, and it was to set the tone of the whole of Josh's life: 'My advice would be to throw him in the pool and make him swim. When he's done that, run his legs off. Make him run round the field, and if he falls over then pick him up and get him to do it again. Exercise is key.'

'Right,' said Josh's dad. 'Then that's what we're going to do.'

It was the founding principle of everything in Josh's life: get out there, get moving, challenge yourself, and don't let yourself be limited or defined by your condition. It was also the start of an incredible relationship between Josh's family and Dr Kramer – by a nice bit of synchronicity, Josh and Dr Kramer shared the same birthday – and Josh's family even invited him for Christmas, causing a bit of confusion when they suddenly realised that the traditional Christmas roast wasn't kosher.

The whole family embraced Dr Kramer's philosophy, even Josh's older brothers, who gave no quarter when it came to rugby tackling him. Luckily, Josh was a naturally sporty child, and took to the rough and tumble like a duck to water. Still, it wasn't easy growing up in the shadow of the condition. Every three months he would have to attend a review, and he was told before he was 16 that he was unlikely to make it to his 30s. 'That has an incredible impact on your life,' he says.

As a child, Josh was so determined not to be seen as different from his friends that he used to hide his tablets, not wanting anyone to know about his condition. He did this so successfully that it wasn't till he was 11 and happened to drop one of his enzyme tablets at the school lunch table that another boy noticed. 'What's that?' he asked. Desperate not to be thought of as somebody with an illness, Josh decided to style it out, and reached for the first thing he could think of.

'Cocaine,' he said, dimly aware from his older brother's conversations that there was a drug of this name.

He might have got away with this – obviously the teachers were well aware of his condition and the medication he needed – if word hadn't got back to the parents: 'Josh Llewellyn-Jones brought cocaine into school?' Fury ensued, and that was the first time in his life that he had to own up to the disease and explain to his classmates what CF was and why he took the tablets.

If there's something rather heartbreaking about the young Josh determined not to let his peers see the full picture of who he was, there's something rather glorious about the time, in his final year at school, when the annual cross-country run rolled around. He had run this five years in a row, and won it every time. As the race approached, one of the other kids went up to the sports teacher to complain.

'Sir, I don't think it's fair that Josh gets to compete in our race any more.'

'Why's that?' said the teacher

'Well, he's got an advantage.'

'What advantage would that be?'

'Well, he's got CF, hasn't he?'

Josh had become so fit that his classmate genuinely believed that having CF conferred extra powers on him. That was definitely a pat on the back for Josh, and didn't do his ego any harm. It was perhaps the first time he was able to think of his condition as a superpower, and the contrast between that and his 11-year-old self sheepishly hiding his tablets every lunchtime showed just how far he had come.

★

The first time I met Josh he was about 17, and was about to go and climb Mount Kilimanjaro. I was doing a piece about it for the Cystic Fibrosis Trust, which is a charity I have been involved with for a long time. Since I'd already climbed it myself, I was pretty intrigued. I had had some breathing issues when I went up, and I'd been pretty fit at the time. So I knew it was going to be some ask. But of course, Josh being Josh, in his own mind merely going up Kilimanjaro wasn't going to be enough. He was already hatching a plan: to have a sparring session at the top of the mountain with a former European heavyweight champion. As you do.

The whole trip had come about because Josh's father had been at a dinner for the CF Trust, and had got talking to some people who happened to have two spaces left on their expedition. Right then and there, Adrian rang Josh and asked if he was up for doing it together, and right then and there, he said yes (you can see where Josh gets his can-do attitude from). Josh's first thought was how fantastic it would be doing something together with his dad, and his next thought, typically, was, 'This is going to be great, but how might we raise even more money?'

It was when he discovered that one of the other people on the team was Scott Welch, a former European heavyweight champion, that the idea for the sparring match took shape. He rang Scott and said, 'I know we haven't met yet, but if you fancy it, shall we have a fight on top of Kilimanjaro, stripped, to raise some more money?'

'Yeah, I'm up for that,' said Scott, 'but how big are you?'

Josh – at the time an extremely lean and wiry 17-year-old due to the cross-country training he did, thought about the enormous Scott, recently retired but still in professional boxer's shape, and didn't miss a beat: 'Don't worry, I'm no threat!' he said.

And that was it. Scott trained him a bit in the basics – how to throw a punch, how to take a punch, and elementary footwork, and the date for the expedition approached.

The plan required a bit of subterfuge. If you've been up Kilimanjaro, you'll know that the porters are quite strict – there are rules up there about what you're allowed to do, and if you have any type of altitude sickness symptoms they take you straight back down again. Scott and Josh put their gloves in their rucksacks and carried them the whole way up. Just before the last ascent – which you start at night, before 11pm, in order to get to the peak before sunrise – Josh had some nosebleeds, a bit of a worry at that altitude. When he came out of his tent with tissue up his nose, Scott looked him up and down and said, 'Looks like you've had a fight already.' But nothing was going to stop Josh reaching his goal.

That final ascent of Kilimanjaro is punishing, as I know from experience. There's a glacier up there, and because you go through the night it's absolutely freezing cold – so cold that the water in your flasks turns to ice so you can't actually drink anything – and pitch-dark. The dark is possibly the worst thing; that and the pace. You cannot begin to imagine how slow that final ascent is, the most painfully slow experience of your life. The porters have this phrase they use, which is 'Pole pole' meaning 'slowly'. All you can see is the lights going up the mountain, and you have no gauge of how far you're getting, so it feels like you are walking forever without making any progress.

I saw some fit and healthy people really struggle; cameramen stumbling and dropping their cameras in tears because they couldn't cope with the altitude. I've seen girls wearing all the clothes that the porters are carrying in an attempt to keep warm still having to turn around and go straight back down at the mountaintop because of the cold. The idea of getting up there, stripping off your layers and having a fight felt insane to me. And the idea of doing all this when you have a condition that limits your lung capacity: it's unimaginable.

But when they reached the top peak, Scott had no sooner looked over to him and said, 'Are you still up for this?' than Josh already had his bag off his back and was stripping down to the waist. The porters thought the two of them were delirious from the altitude: 'Hey, what's going on? What are you doing?'

They had only meant to box for a couple of minutes, but when they started throwing punches, a circle formed round them, and Josh realised out of the corner of his eye that a camera was trained on them. He decided that he couldn't go home not having tried to land a proper punch, so he hit Scott in the face as hard as he could. Scott didn't move: he just looked at Josh, shook his head and came in to give him one swift clip on the nose, which of course exploded into a nosebleed. None of this deterred them, though, and they carried on sparring. In the photos there is the tiny Josh, the enormous Scott, against this amazing backdrop. It was quite a moment. Josh didn't even rest there – he took the opportunity of being at the top of the mountain to hit a golf ball just to see how far it would go, and again for charity did 100 keep-ups. Altogether, they ended up raising £140,000. Josh's passion for raising money for charity was born.

I love to think about Josh up there, on a mountain at the top of the world, behaving – in the best possible way – like an absolute idiot, throwing punches and doing his keep-ups, raising over £100,000 for charity, and most of all sharing the experience with his dad, who had always done so much for him and who turned 60 on that trip. 'It was just magical, you know, I shared a tear at the top with him. Well, I say that: I don't know if it was just that Scott hit me so hard I started crying...'

★

CF or no CF, this was a young man at the peak of his game. Cut to a scene three years later, though, and Josh's character was about to be tested in a whole different way. He was 21, and physically quite changed from the wiry teenager I had first met. He had got into weightlifting – probably to impress women, he admits – and become really strong. He felt invincible. One afternoon, helping his parents move house, he lifted up a washing machine on his own without waiting for help. As he put it down, he felt something shift and go pop inside him, and lifting up his T-shirt, he realised that a lump was protruding from his abdomen. It was too painful for him to touch himself, so he turned to his brother and asked him to push on it for him. Cue Josh hitting the deck, curled into a foetal position around the pain.

He was blue-lighted to hospital, and after the scans had been done, at about 6pm, with the family gathered round his bed, the surgeon told him that they would have to operate: 'We've looked at your records and it's not looking too good.' He added one sentence that would stay with Josh for a long time: 'You might want to say goodbye to your family.'

As Josh puts it now, 'I don't mind admitting that at that point I had a pretty big ego. I'd won all my cross-country races, all the Welsh national races, I was a cross-country champion, captain of my local football team. I'd been on trial with Cardiff City, played rugby to a high level, was pretty good at all the sports I turned my hand to. But that one line – "call your family" – took that ego from me straight away. I grew up pretty quick on that bed, that night.'

He focused on not letting his parents know just how scared he was, on making sure he didn't cry in front of them. He was wheeled down the long, long corridor, with his mother on one side, his dad on the other and his brothers walking behind. When they reached the swing doors at the end, his mum kissed him on the forehead, and he tried for one last joke: 'I'm not dead yet, you don't have to kiss me on the forehead.' Nobody laughed.

Then he said goodbye and was wheeled through the doors, and waited until they had swung shut behind him before the tears came. 'If I go tonight,' he said to the anaesthetist, 'please don't let anyone know I cried. I don't want them to know how scared I was.' That was his last memory before the countdown to the anaesthetic started.

Seven and a half hours later he woke up as though in a movie: there was a circular bright light and two heads hovering above him. When he looked down his body, he saw blood, staples and a colostomy bag, and let out a scream. That scream was the first indication to his father, pacing the corridor outside, that Josh was still alive. It turned out that he had a massive blockage in his stomach. The cause stemmed back to the very first day of his life. When the doctors back then had found the blood-filled abscess and operated, their main focus had been to get him back to his family for what might have been his final hours. It meant that when they put his intestines back in and sewed him up, the intestines weren't put in exactly as they had been, so Josh had grown up with chronic stomach pains. Unfortunately, being the kind of person he was, and living with the symptoms of CF, Josh assumed that this pain was just one more part of the condition and had never questioned it. So he had lived with twisted intestines for 21 years, until they brought him to this operating room. It was, said the doctors, as though a bomb had gone off in his stomach.

Josh had lived with CF and all that went with it for his entire life, but it was perhaps this ordeal that most profoundly changed him. Up to this point, he was, as he would happily admit himself, probably pretty cocky.

But suddenly everything changed. He went from being in the best shape of his life, a natural athlete, ready for anything, to somebody who was full of fear: 'My confidence went from arrogance to literally not wanting to go outside.' He was in the kind of pain that even someone with his high threshold found almost unbearable. For two months, he was confined to a sofa, but even once he was moving he couldn't find his old spirit. It was the colostomy bag that in some ways symbolised his mental state: it was something he found 'shattering'. He cancelled holidays, unable to bear the thought of stripping down to his shorts. When his friends wanted to tempt him outside to kick a ball around, he remembers, 'The only way I could do it was to wear one of those long-sleeve skin tops that would keep the bag really tight to me, and then a really baggy T-shirt over the top and then sometimes a hoody as well, because my confidence was at an all-time low. I didn't want anyone to know.' The knowledge that he might have to have the bag for life was something that plunged him into despair. Even when they decided he could have the surgery to reverse the colostomy, the journey was far from over. The operation was repeatedly delayed. On one occasion when he was actually in a hospital bed waiting for the procedure, a nurse came in to inform him that the surgery had been bumped and he would have to wait another three months. It was a long, hard road to recovery, both physically and mentally. What Josh felt most of all was a mixture of despair and anger; he had worked so hard to keep the monkey of CF off his back, he'd made sure he was super-fit, had done all the right things, and yet all the same it had come so close to finishing him off. It took him several years to get properly back on track.

It was strange, because Josh had lived his whole life with a serious and chronic condition. Since the day he was born he had been told that his life was limited. Yet it wasn't until this horrific experience that this sense of mortality was brought home to him. He freely admits that in spite of his CF he had been relatively lucky with his health – yes, he had to take endless pills and do his physiotherapy, but where some children with CF are regularly hospitalised for infections, up to the age of 17 he had only had to have one long stint in hospital for IVs. That had been an uncomfortable two weeks, but it was something he could shrug off. This was different. Now the import of what he had always been told – that he might not reach his 30th birthday – really hit home. Something in him shifted. Slowly he came round to a different viewpoint. There was an urgency that he hadn't felt before; a niggle in his mind saying that whatever he wanted to do, he had to do it now.

Up to this point, Josh had loved the charity fundraising he had done, but as he himself would admit, a big part of the motivation for him was the thrill of doing cool stuff and pushing his own limits. But after this, his attitude changed; he realised he had a chance to make a real difference, and to see what he could achieve for others, and what he could help others achieve: 'I'll die when I die, but I want to make sure that even if I have a short life it's going to be a good one.' He realised the necessity of making the most of every day, quite literally: 'My view was right, now I've got to do something serious because running a marathon isn't enough any more… I've really got to push myself.' Most importantly, he understood that raising money wasn't the real gift he was giving CF children. The question that was burning in his mind was 'How do I empower CF children today to grow up understanding that there are no limits?' Thanks to his parents and Dr Bob Kramer this was the way he had been raised, and he realised that what he most wanted was to give this same gift to other children with CF: 'Throughout my life I've always had limits put on me. I've always had doctors saying you can't do this, or you're never going to do that. And I've always been like, "sod that". So how do I show the world, and particularly the CF community, what's truly possible if you can set your mind to it?'

The answer, he realised, was to do things that were so huge and eye-catching that they couldn't be ignored. If he could be up there with the best, breaking world records, then everyone would see that there were no limits. 'I want kids with CF, wherever they are in the world, to know you can be the best in the world at something, whatever you put your mind to. You don't have to lift weights, you don't have to do these stupid exercise regimes that I do, but just put your mind to something, achieve what you want to achieve with your life.'

As Josh's 30th birthday approached, he decided he wanted to mark it in real style. He had grown up with doctors saying he wouldn't survive past 30, and now he had reached the milestone, he wanted to celebrate it hard. For him, of course, this meant doing something for charity. Searching online, he discovered the World's Fittest Man challenge. This had only been completed by a tiny handful of people at this point, and Josh wanted to be the next. It's not surprising so few people have completed it. The challenge means having to lift 100 tons, cycle 100 miles, run 10 miles, row 10 miles, cross-train 10 miles, swim 2 miles, then do 3,000 situps, 1,000 press-ups and 1,000 squats. All this, in 24 hours. Two short three-minute breaks are allowed, and no more. I know, it feels tiring just to read about it.

When his dad asked why he wanted to do something so extreme, Josh's answer was immediate: 'That's what it's going to take to show the CF community that truly anything is possible, something bonkers like that.' The extreme nature of the challenge was the whole point – and also the best way to persuade people to dig into their pockets for a good cause.

It won't surprise you to hear that Josh succeeded in becoming the fifth person ever to complete the World's Fittest Man challenge, managing to do it in 22 hours 10 minutes.. As he finished, completely knackered but feeling amazing, his trainer turned to him and said, 'That's great, Josh, but the thing is, you're live on Facebook, and you've promised all these kids you're going to exercise for 24 hours non-stop, what are you going to do now?' So he jumped on the rowing machine and did another ten miles, just to keep going and fulfil the promise he had made.

Completing that challenge was made particularly special by the presence of Dr Bob Kramer, who in spite of age and ill health had made the trip over from Dallas to be there: it was extraordinary to be able to complete this feat in the presence of this man whose advice all those years before had set the course of his life. Two days later they had a joint birthday party, and Dr Bob said to him, 'Well, that challenge was great, but you've said to everyone you're going to do an annual challenge, so what's next?' Dr Bob would sadly pass away a few weeks after this, leaving Josh forever grateful to have had that last encounter with the man who changed his life.

★

The answer to Dr Bob's question didn't come immediately, but in his heart Josh knew that it would have to involve weightlifting, which is his passion. Discovering that the current weightlifting world record holder was a man who had lifted

475,000 kilos in 24 hours, Josh sat down, did some maths, and said to his father, 'I'm going to beat this guy's record.'

'Great,' said his dad. 'Half a million kilos sounds amazing.'

But to Josh, that wasn't going to be enough: 'If we're going to get decent press and raise decent awareness, then half a million doesn't have the right ring to it. It has to be a million.'

A million kilos in 24 hours? That would require him to lift at least 700kg every minute – or in fact more, when you factor in eating and toilet breaks. The first problem was how to train for something like that: it's never been done, so there's no roadmap. He was offered training by some ex-SAS soldiers, who started off by putting him through the most intense fitness session that even Josh had ever taken part in. After three hours, at the point where he was throwing up from exhaustion, they said, 'That's great, that's the warm-up done, now let's get to work.' It was a test: Jay and Kyle needed to know that Josh had the drive and commitment to see the next 12 months of training through, because they knew just how tough it was going to have to be.

And tough it was: seven hours a day lifting weights, with just one day off in every ten, for a year. Two weeks before the challenge, in 2018, he found he was unable to lift a kettle to make himself a cup of coffee with his right hand. It turned out that he had developed stress fractures in three of the bones – they were crumbling from the inside. There was nothing to do but plough on: the doctor didn't feel comfortable giving steroid injections under the circumstances, and Josh's digestive issues ruled out taking painkillers. An ITV crew were coming to film, the press was all teed up. Josh took ten days off from lifting in the days before, and determined to power through.

On the day, his trainer came over to him: 'Have you practised using your hand yet?' he said.

'No,' said Josh, so his trainer ushered him to a bench, where he tried one rep. 'OK, I think I can do it,' he said. 'Just don't tape up the hand, because that will make me think about it.' Instead, they used iced water every hour to numb it, only resorting to tape when the pain became too much.

After ten hours Josh hit the world record point – but that was less than half of his goal. He had another fourteen hours to go. It involved all his reserves of strength, his team carrying him between the weight stations because his legs gave way, quite a few sick buckets, and some very dark hours, but in the end, he did it. Another record smashed.

Over the years Josh has continued to put his mind and body to the test. In 2019 he swam the length of the English Channel, cycled 200 miles to St James's Palace in London – where Prince Charles had kindly laid on the best lasagne of his life – before running the 160 miles from London to Cardiff. The whole challenge took five days with no rest, but after a gruelling last leg, where he injured his ankle and had to hobble the last 80 miles, he finished up triumphantly in Cardiff's Principality Stadium. In 2021, he completed the 24-hour squat challenge, and four weeks later ran for 24 hours without stopping.

It sometimes seems nothing can slow Josh down, but it's easy when talking about his amazing feats to skate over the extreme demands he is placing on his body. Cystic fibrosis can weaken the bones, so he has to be more careful about the stress fractures that such concentrated exercise can bring. It may not look like it, but nowadays he is careful to ensure that he doesn't go too far: 'For me, it's about fun, making it enjoyable.' Superhuman he may be, but he wants to be a little bit careful with the body he has.

Having said that, a few weeks after I last spoke to him, in his constant pursuit of living life to its fullest Josh went head over heels over the handlebars of a mountain bike. He broke four ribs, cracked his collarbone and punctured his lung. It meant another hospital stay, made worse when he picked up a lung infection and had to be put on morphine. He is undeterred though: four weeks afterwards, having ditched the morphine, he is on the road to recovery, missing his exercise regime but making up for it with a well-deserved holiday.

That attitude is part and parcel of who he is. For me, Josh is a hero not just because he has raised so much money for charity – over £800,000 at the time of writing – but because the very way he lives his life is an inspiration. His refusal to set limits to his achievements means that he has expanded the boundaries of what is possible.

Perhaps this is best embodied by the charity he and his brother set up, CF Warriors. The rationale behind CF Warriors is a simple one: he wanted to do for other kids with the condition what Dr Bob had done for him all those years ago: encourage them to be as fit and active as they could possibly be. He wanted to do something that would bring families living with CF together and promote a healthy, positive attitude. He had in his mind that if he could change the outlook of just one family, one child with CF, that would be enough.

To know he had helped someone have a better life, whether that meant a happier life, a longer life, or a healthier one. The charity has sent out over 500 packs to children all over the world – America, Australia, Europe. Within days of it starting, they found themselves overwhelmed with the enthusiasm of the response.

His aim was that any family who had just discovered that their child has CF should find the CF Warrior community, and feel hope: 'I want them to find the positivity. I want them to find the right mindset that will genuinely help them tackle this thing.' Josh is adamant that this attitude starts with the parents. He believes that children are only limited by what they've been told is their limits: 'So it's not just about empowering kids, it's about empowering adults to positively promote exercise in a fun environment that keeps kids doing it for longer.' He wants CF Warriors to show families a different way to live with CF. When parents come to him, worried about how to encourage exercise in their children, his advice is simple: 'Do something fun, just do something fun. Don't see it as we have to go run a mile or run a 5k, just go have fun with your child, and move.'

CF Warriors is more than just a charity, it's a community. The community aspect is hugely important because a particularly cruel aspect of the condition is that it can be dangerous for people with cystic fibrosis to spend time together because of the risk of cross infection. It is a horrible irony that the thing that sets them apart also keeps them apart. Growing up, that meant Josh didn't know anyone who was going through the same as he was. Brilliant as his family were, there was nobody he could talk to who could fully relate to the problems he was going through. Social media could be a gamechanger here, Josh realised. With CF Warriors he could create an environment where kids could make friends online in a safe environment, with their parents involved: 'In the end, it's not me helping them, they're all helping each other.' Each member gets a hoody, a hat, a T-shirt, CF Warrior pill boxes and wristbands. Putting on the kit, they are putting on armour – joining a brilliantly positive, encouraging, enthusiastic tribe.

For Josh, there is nothing better than receiving a video message from a kid proudly decked out in his CF Warriors gear, or hearing that on a school 'Wear your own clothes' day they have chosen their CF Warrior hoody. One child, asked to do a presentation on superheroes for their school homework, chose Josh.

Josh's social media feed – full to the brim with pictures of insanely early starts, punishing training regimes, and wholesome-looking, early-morning swims – also regularly features videos of him taking his tablets. CF Warrior families have been known to use these to get their kids to take their tablets, using TikTok to make it into a duet. That 11-year-old kid who hid his medication for the whole of primary school has definitely come a long way: the medication is now out and proud. The message is: embrace your life.

★

Many years ago, one of Josh's classmates thought that having CF gave Josh some kind of an advantage. The idea seemed laughable at the time. But looking at his life now, Josh has come to have a different perspective than he had as a child: 'I've come to realise it is an advantage, because I look at life completely differently to all my mates. Actually, without it I probably wouldn't be as resilient, I wouldn't be as physically able... I genuinely believe it's because I've been forced to exercise to stay healthy. I'm lucky that I love it, but CF has forced me to be who I am.'

I've been lucky enough to know Josh since he was a skinny teenager, and have watched him grow into a force of nature. You come away from any encounter with Josh bowled over by his positivity. He is full of life, ambition and focus, the antithesis of what you expect of someone who is dealing with a difficult, draining and life-limiting illness. His superpower is not that he has had the strength to take his challenges and turn them into positives; it is that he has the ability to make others feel the same way. One of Josh's favourite sayings is: 'Impossible is not a fact, it's an opinion'. After meeting him, it's easy to believe that.

Charlie Martin

When Charlie Martin was a child, her great ambition was to be a fighter pilot. That's probably not that unusual for someone who was a tomboyish type with two older brothers at home. She was a pretty happy-go-lucky kid, not that sporty but always active, who spent her time climbing trees and playing soldiers, and whose favourite film was *Top Gun*. The problem was that while being a fighter pilot was her dream, she was pretty sure she would never become one. Why? Because the other thing she knew about herself was that although she had been assigned male at birth, this felt completely wrong to her. From an early age, she just knew that actually she was a woman. So even when, slightly later on, she discovered that it might be possible to transition, her first thought was, well, if that happened, what am I going to do for a job? As Charlie puts it now, almost shocked that this was the reality, trans people seemed to be either impossibly glamorous drag presences in films, or involved in the sex industry in some way. And neither of those looked very likely or attractive for someone growing up in suburban Leicestershire.

Nowadays, Charlie is not a fighter pilot. Instead, she is a very successful racing driver, making waves in the endurance car-racing circuit. Her daily life involves speed, petrol, racetracks and adrenaline; not to mention podiums, trophies and brand partnerships. She has driven the Michelin Le Mans Cup, and last year took part in the 24 Hours of Nürburgring race. Glamorous and great fun (and occasionally terrifying) as her Instagram page makes it all look, there is no doubting that it has taken tons of hard work, ambition and dedication to get herself to this point. Her ultimate dream now is to take part in the prestigious 24 Hours of Le Mans, and I have no doubt she's going to make it. Most importantly of all, she is able to be herself.

Thinking back to the limitations she saw on her life when she was young in the eighties and nineties, she can hardly believe that that was her thinking. 'It's so bizarre to me now that that was the scope of my imagination at that point,' she says. 'But that was the reality because that was what it was like back then. You didn't see anything else.'

Which is why it is so important that people like Charlie are now flying the flag, showing that it is possible for anybody to live their true selves while following their dreams in any walk of life.

★

I first encountered Charlie when I was presenting *Ninja Warrior UK* in 2018. On that particular course there was an obstacle – the I-Beam – that was incredibly difficult. It was the second-last obstacle, before the infamous wall, and it involved gripping tightly onto the ever-narrowing sides of an I-Beam that had a right-angle bend halfway down. Contestant after contestant was getting round the course, reaching the I-Beam, and dropping into the water hazard below. Then all of a sudden, well over halfway through, this very glamorous blonde woman hit the course. We knew she was a racing driver, so I guess we thought she would have the competitive spirit, but it was absolutely jaw-droppingly impressive the way she hit that obstacle. It involved huge amounts of strength in the hands and arms, and I just remember Charlie hanging on for dear life, ascending the first part vertically and then gripping on upside down on the horizontal portion, just refusing to let it defeat her. The cheers in the studio as she nonchalantly jumped off it at the end, then faced the Wall and stormed up it in one swift movement nearly took the roof off. It was an amazing moment, not only for her but for everyone cheering her on. The whole place was just blown away.

That might have been that, if it hadn't been for a conversation I had a month or two later with one of my best mates. He was telling me that the sister of one of his oldest friends had been on the show and had done brilliantly. 'I didn't know Ian had any sisters,' I said, as I put it together. And he told me about Charlie's story and that she was not only a fantastic racing driver, but the only transgender racing driver on the circuit. I don't mind admitting that I was floored by this, because I simply had no idea. On the show, we had simply thought of Charlie as who she is – glamorous racing driver and fabulously determined contestant. At the time, Charlie didn't choose to make her story part of the show. It's something I totally understand – television can be fast-paced and want to hit solely the headline points, and there are only a few moments to tell the contestants' stories. A female racing driver was enough to get to grips with; I can see why she didn't feel she had the space to tell her whole story. Not to mention the fact that she wasn't fully out in the tough world of motor racing at that point.

In fact, 2018 was the year that she came out definitively and publicly, something that 'was a big leap of faith', as she puts it. It's possible, she thinks now, that having that moment of triumph on the show, in front of millions and millions of people, gave her the impetus to come out fully. Whether that is true or not, even a glance at her Instagram now – an equal mix of petrol-head's dream, fantastic adrenaline-spiked travels, and touchingly frank videos about her transition and the issues close to her heart as a trans person – is enough to convince you that she is finally living the life she could never have dreamed of but which she definitely deserves.

Charlie realised she was trans early on in life – at around six or seven years old. That is, she knew she had been born into the wrong body, but she had no name for how she felt at that time. Not least because there was nobody either in her own life or on the wider stage who seemed to represent those feelings. As she puts it, 'Everything I'd see on the subject on television is basically saying this is weird, it's wrong, it's negative, it's not acceptable: that was a real conundrum to wrestle with.'

Charlie can still remember, in technicolour, the first time she ever saw anyone on television who seemed to represent something of what she felt. This was Caroline Cossey, probably the most high-profile trans person in the eighties. She was a Bond girl, a model, a hugely glamorous figure. 'It just blew my mind... like Wow, this is actually a thing. There are other people who feel like this – you can be born one way and you transition.' That was a revelation. But the high-octane film star life still seemed a million miles away from anything Charlie could aspire to. Then there was RuPaul being interviewed on *The Word*, which was fantastic, but it all seemed to be impossibly distant. There didn't seem to be a way to reconcile these larger-than-life personalities with the kind of existence that she was living.

Nevertheless, at the age of around 11, Charlie took the brave step of coming out to a few schoolfriends, and then to her mother – she told her just before she was going away for a weekend, which maybe gave her mum time to process it, but also meant that when she got back it felt 'really, really awkward to talk to her because Mum was always the easiest person to talk to about anything.' Her mum was supportive, kind and understanding, but confused. She found it hard to compute that her tree-climbing, tomboyish son had this completely different internal identity. Charlie had never seemed to want to play with dolls or to wear dresses, so it came out of the blue for her mum. ('I was like, "Well, I don't have any dolls and I don't have any dresses 'cause I've got two older brothers!"' says Charlie.)

Again, the lack of real trans visibility was a huge hurdle for the young Charlie in trying to explain where she thought she might fit in. 'There was no context... You could say today, "Well look, here are some people on Instagram who live very alternative lifestyles..."' But back then, there was just nothing she could point to – she was having to explain this incredibly complex thing with very few handholds or reference points. That early lack of role models is a huge reason why she so proudly drives in her rainbow-adorned helmet now, and why she is so upfront and high-profile about her story: 'That's the power of people who are visible doing what they're doing. And I guess that's a big driver for me in terms of coming out in my industry. Sometimes it takes people to blaze that trail and create that change, to try and build that environment for other people. It's a big part of the motivation of what gets me out of bed in the morning.'

Social media, of course, can be a double-edged sword. While it can be a huge source of inspiration and comfort to people who are trying to find their identities, we all know that opening up online can absolutely mean laying yourself open to the worst forms of attack. And Charlie has definitely seen both sides of this: 'On the one hand, getting a lot of validation from the community you belong to, which is an amazing thing and had huge benefits in terms of my confidence. But you are also opening yourself up to the negativity.' It is lucky that Charlie now lives such a full and busy life – she can allow the negative comments to slide off her to some extent. Nevertheless, there are moments, such as the one recently when she did a promotion on German television, which led to people saying they would boycott the company, that still take her aback. Charlie's life may look enviable, but she has definitely not taken an easy path.

★

After that early coming out to her mother, Charlie grew up while continuing to live as a man, getting into motor racing at a grassroots level in the UK after she left university, and doing it on a shoestring by buying and outfitting her first car all by herself. But the split between who she really was and the way she was forcing herself to live was becoming unbearable. It's so strange, talking to the wonderfully measured, confident, articulate and clearly content Charlie now, to know that at one stage it felt like the darkness was overwhelming her.

It was at that stage, in 2012, that she took the huge step of deciding to transition. In fact, in making that decision she more or less assumed that in doing so she would have to give up the sport she loved. But she was drawn back in, with friends and family knowing that it was what made her happy. Re-entering that space, where everybody had known her as a man, was perhaps the most terrifying part of her journey. It was the support of her friends on the circuit – who had known her before her transition, but were totally accepting of her re-entry into the sport as a woman – that buoyed her up and got her through.

It's no secret that the motor racing world is a pretty testosterone-heavy, male-driven environment. There was definitely a fear that in going properly public with her story she might be endangering the career she had done so much to build up. How much has Charlie come up against overt discrimination in her job? While it hasn't been without its challenges, she has mostly had quite a positive experience. Like any other woman in an industry that is dominated by men, she knows she probably puts herself under a bit more pressure in order to prove herself: she is usually the one who is turning up a day early on the track to get to know the team, or putting in the extra effort so that people will see that she is totally committed. But then, that is part of being a good teammate.

The position she occupies in the sport was summed up for

her perhaps in an experience she once had after joining a new team. After their first race she and a teammate stood on the podium together, and he told her later that he had overheard some guys saying some negative things about her being trans. This wasn't a total surprise – Charlie knows that there are things people say behind her back that mightn't be said to her face (hence the cesspool that social media can be). But the main thing she takes away from that story is that her teammate had her back, stepping in and calling them out on it. Considering she had only known him a few days at that point, she thought that was 'pretty cool'. And she knows too that just by being there and being herself and standing on that podium, she is making an impact.

★

In the years since I first met her on *Ninja Warrior,* I have interviewed Charlie a couple of times, and she has always flown the flag with such pride and articulacy. I wonder whether she sometimes would prefer that the strapline every time she races didn't have to be 'transgender racing driver', but for the moment, she knows that it is so important that she should be out there and visible. 'Yeah, in an ideal world I would just be "Charlie Martin, racing driver", but I'm proud of who I am and being trans is part of who I am. It's part of my story, it's part of my journey and I'm proud of the journey I've gone through to be where I am. And also, we're not there yet. We need people who are prepared to put their head above the parapet and have shots fired at them if it means achieving more progress.'

For the moment, things are getting better, but there is still a long way to go. For Charlie, a perfect world would look like one 'Where people just have a greater level of awareness and understanding and empathy, and where we don't feel as a community of people that we are constantly having to fight for validation in society.'

Until then, everything Charlie does – her successes on the track, her constant advocacy for trans rights, the many ways she speaks up for her community and her visibility in a walk of life that up till now has been anything but diverse – provides an amazing example to anybody who feels they don't fit in. Everything about her life paints a totally different picture to what was available when she was young, with 'the complete absence of any kind of trans role models. There were no trans people in sport racing cars, there was no one I could look to as a kid and think, Brilliant, that's what I want to be, that's who I'm going to be like and that's what I'm going to aim for.'

I ask her what she would say to herself, if she could, back when she was that young child who couldn't understand their own place in the world. 'I'd say, "Don't feel like you need to have everything worked out and a perfect explanation of who you want to be and what that looks like... don't feel you have to get everything right. It's all about taking small steps and learning as you go. Just do what feels right for you, and not what you think other people expect you to do and who other people expect you to be."'

It's pretty good advice for all of us, I reckon. And I'm also sure that if out there somewhere is another young trans kid who dreams of speed, just the knowledge that they could be as fabulous as Charlie will be a hell of an inspiration.

Candoco

Something you might not know about me is that back in the day I was a dance student: I did my BA in contemporary dance at Birmingham University. I have to admit I stumbled into this degree almost by accident. I was a sports-mad rugby player, and originally I thought I was applying for a degree in drama. So you can imagine the scene at the audition. There we were at the barre – 16 girls in tights and leotards, and right in the middle, me in my grubby rugby shorts. Luckily, I'd got a friend of my mum's who was a dance teacher to take me through the basics the day before: first, second and third position, a little bit of jazz, a bit of contemporary, and some step ball changes, but I still must have looked like something out of a comedy sketch. I managed to get in, but I mention all this to explain that my expertise in the world of dance was pretty poor at the time I started my studies. Up until then, I had never properly seen any ballet or contemporary dance, and when I did, it just blew my mind.

In particular, I had never properly appreciated how physically impressive the dancers were. For someone who was as sporty and active as I was, this was a revelation. The women were long and elegant and graceful, with a strength that came from their sinews and bones and muscles, but the men were just jaw-droppingly amazing. I remember seeing a company called Motion House for the first time and being absolutely overawed. It was a whole new way of understanding what bodies could do – the power and strength and physicality, juxtaposed with the elegance and the softness with which they could move, and the poise with which they crossed the stage. There was one dancer doing a routine where he held himself up alongside a tall fridge, suspending himself only with the power of one arm flat out from his side while he danced in mid-air: the strength needed to hold himself up that way, just by forcing his arm down, was astonishing. I was spellbound.

That was a pretty brilliant time, all in all: I loved my degree – again, it was me and 16 girls in leotards and tights: what's not to love? – and I met my wife there (she was doing philosophy). Naturally I remember a lot of messing about and going to pubs and making friends. But actually, as dance students, we worked really hard too. As well as the practical element, we had a huge number of lectures and essays – more than the nurses, in fact. And we had to write a dissertation. For the purposes of this book, I dug mine out of the attic recently. It's called '8 dancers, 14 legs, 6 wheels and a bicycle pump: A recipe for success?' and it was an analysis of what was then, and still is, a groundbreaking and fascinating dance company: Candoco. This was a company unlike any other at the time, one that brought together able-bodied and disabled dancers in world-class contemporary dance performances.

I fell in love with them then, and now, 30 years later, I can see even more clearly the significance of what they were doing. Candoco changed not only the world of dance and how it sees disabled people, but also how they are perceived in wider society. In other words, they are absolutely the definition of trailblazers. It's woven into their DNA, right from their conception.

★

Candoco came about almost organically, as the result of a collaboration between the dancer Celeste Dandekar and the choreographer Adam Benjamin. Celeste, who had been on track for a stellar career in contemporary dance, had been left with radical spinal injuries after a catastrophic on-stage accident in 1973. She was only 21, and it seemed as though her dancing life was over, but she continued to be connected to that world through her work as a costume designer, and in 1990 she made a piece of work with the dancer and choreographer Darshan Singh Bhuller, called *The Fall*. This was an extraordinary short film, shot in black and white, in which the two of them dance together – an incredibly emotive piece which conveys Celeste's own innate expressiveness of movement, and explores the psychological impact of what had happened to her.

It was after that ground-breaking piece that she and Adam Benjamin, a dancer and choreographer who was involved with the spinal injury charity Aspire, where she was a trustee, came together. They started an evening class which in turn led to a series of residencies and workshops, including one at the Northern School of Contemporary Dance. Throughout this process other dancers and choreographers, both disabled and non-disabled, came on board. These included Lea Parkinson,

Helen Baggett, John French, and David Toole, a fantastic dancer with no legs who would go on to have an extraordinary career. At this point, though, he was a postman, who it later transpired had come along to a workshop at the Northern School of Contemporary Dance as a dare. Also at those workshops was Charlotte Darbyshire, who was then training at NSCD, and who now, 30 years later, is artistic director of the company. The seeds of what would become Candoco were sown.

The piece they developed in those workshops got a standing ovation when they performed it at NSCD. It 'took the roof off', in Charlotte's words, and led to an invitation to perform it at the South Bank in London. Once again, the reception was rapturous, and it was out of the reaction to that performance that Candoco was born.

Candoco. I love the way that even the name itself captures exactly what a trailblazing hero does: 'A focus on what we *can* do rather than what we can't, which had been the experience of a lot of disabled people,' as Charlotte puts it.

Having had the privilege of learning all about Candoco at first-hand back in 1997 – this was about six years after they had been founded – I find myself feeling rather emotional at the chance of talking to Charlotte today. I've been loosely keeping track of them since then – I've seen their ground-breaking performances on *Strictly Come Dancing* and at the Paralympic Games opening and closing ceremonies – but my life has taken me rather far from my days of dancing and it's been a long time since I went through the rigorous mental workout of talking about dance.

But it turns out that a conversation with Charlotte is a truly wonderful experience – partly because she is such a thoughtful and interesting person, and partly because our conversation reminds me – on an intellectual, emotional, psychological and simply human level – just what I loved about Candoco in the first place.

With a 30-year history with the company, Charlotte has an exceptional perspective on the company itself, and on the shifting landscape it exists in. I ask her about the very beginnings, and she remembers those early workshops as a hugely exciting time, one where, as she puts it, able-bodied and disabled dancers 'were genuinely working out how we might move together, and we quickly discovered that what we could do together was so much richer than either of us could do apart.'

That statement – that in coming together the dancers were creating something far greater than any of them could create in their separate experiences – is the philosophy that lies at the absolute heart of the whole company. I'd go so far as to say it contains a lesson for life itself.

What Candoco were doing was referred to as 'integrated' dance – that is, dance that integrated able-bodied and differently abled people. But that concept was almost entirely new. Really, the perception of dance for disabled people, if there was one at all, was limited to the idea of dance as a therapeutic activity, not as an art form. From the very beginning, the founders not only wanted to challenge that idea but to blow it out of the water. 'Because of Celeste's experience of dance and her connections, it was really important for her that we were positioned in the mainstream, and we held our own alongside any other regular dance company,' Charlotte says. They wanted to produce work that was challenging, that would be intellectually and aesthetically stimulating, that would be performed on the world's best contemporary dance stages, and that would attract the most renowned of choreographers and collaborators. Their first two collaborators, Emilyn Claid and Siobhan Davies, were world-class. Candoco had staked out the kind of territory they would be operating in, and they went on to work with everyone from hugely established choreographers to emerging new talents.

That was more or less where they were when I encountered them in 1997: a fresh, challenging, invigorating presence in the world of contemporary dance. But that description doesn't really convey quite the impact they had on me back then. Remember, it had not been that long since I had had my eyes opened to what dance could be, full stop. And now all of a sudden I was watching something completely different. I was seeing a serious contemporary dance company with all the physical prowess and perfectionism that entailed, but one in which the bodies I was looking at came in completely different shapes and forms.

This was a dramatic handbrake turn on my conception of what dance was. To watch Candoco perform and move and fit together, this mesmeric integration of people with wheelchairs, limb differences, and archetypal bodies, gave me an entirely new and exciting perspective. I realised it wasn't just about power, strength and athleticism – the grace and mobility of a dancer could just as easily come from the spinning or leaning of a wheelchair, or the fall of a body, or someone with a limb difference creating an unexpected shape as they formed a mirror with someone with two arms. Suddenly I was evaluating movement and performance in a whole new way, but I could see that the beauty and the narrative and the drama and the pain and the joy of what they were doing was just the same. Appreciating that was so important for me, not just as part of my understanding of dance, but really of understanding life. I think it was probably the first time I really started to value what disability can mean for people who are trying to face the same world as me but from a different perspective. Learning about dance had been exciting for me. This opened my eyes a second time, but in a way that was so much more important. For that, I will always be grateful to Candoco.

Let's stand back for a second and look at the wider landscape into which Candoco was born. There simply wasn't the same conversation about people with different abilities in those days. Reading back through my dissertation now, in 2022, there are moments where my jaw falls open. As part of the research, I had sent out a questionnaire to various people in the dance world, asking them about their experience of Candoco and the work they were doing. Here is the response I got from one dance critic: 'I'm sorry, Ben, I cannot help. I have not written about Candoco. Although I think it's absolutely wonderful for them to enjoy the dance experience, I prefer not to look.' *I prefer not to look.* Quite apart from the pat-on-the-head condescension of the idea of people with different bodies 'enjoying the dance experience' – remember, we are talking about serious and highly trained dance professionals here – this was a landscape in which someone could comfortably write such a thing down, sign their name to it and send it off to be part of someone's academic dissertation. It feels like another planet.

When I relay this to Charlotte (it feels ridiculously rude even to read it out to her), she rolls her eyes a bit, but is 'sadly not shocked'. As a company, particularly in those early days, that kind of thing was par for the course. They used their sense of humour and their closeness as a company to take such things in their stride: 'We were able to read those early critiques with dismay but also dismiss them,' she says now. She reckons that the company had been going for about ten years before a review properly tackled the work on an artistic level, rather than reaching for the disability narrative. The most common treatment was the 'brave-and-tragic, aren't they wonderful?, poor things' trope. Critics and film crews reporting on the company liked to focus in particular on David Toole, whose radical disability fed most obviously into this angle, something that was hard both on him and the rest of the company.

As for audiences, there were moments when people walked out of performances. And there was often an audible gasp when David ran across the stage on his hands. 'While he was sat out of his chair I think people assumed there was a hole in the floor,' says Charlotte. I remember as a dancer that in general you'd much rather that the audience have a sharp intake of breath than sit there indifferent, so I guess challenging those responses was part of what the company was all about: they were, after all, 'trying to smash up some assumptions'. Still, it must at times have been tiring to try and keep focused on the art form in the face of these reactions.

★

Nowadays, things look rather different. Since those early days of barely being paid and scrambling for Arts Council funding, Candoco have put themselves on the map. They have worked with world-class collaborators, and have built up an archive of over 50 works. They perform on the world's leading stages, from Sadler's Wells in London to the Brooklyn Academy of Music in New York. To get a sense of where they are artistically, take the recent collaboration they did on that stage, where they took on an absolutely seminal work, *Set and Reset* by the revered choreographer Trisha Brown. They reimagined it from the ground up, to produce *Set and Reset/Reset*.

The original *Set and Reset* was innovative in the way that it combined a mesmerically intricate piece of dance with revolutionary set design, lighting and music to produce something that was a highly layered and complicated experience for the audience. It was almost an assault on the senses. There was so much to look at, so many changes of focus, right down to the way that the set had transparent wings so that even when the dancers were offstage, they were still on. It's a piece that at times was almost claustrophobic – the dancers moved so closely together, then spun away suddenly to be in time with someone else, or performed a movement that matched with a dancer across the stage. The complication and flow and rhythm of their movement had to be perfectly timed. Taking this multi-layered experience, and adding in a wheelchair, or a dancer with limb difference, takes it to yet another level. To watch a body that is missing a limb mirroring a conventional one, or focus on the swing of an artificial arm, adds a fascinating extra texture. It's something absolutely bewitching and hypnotic. I could watch it for hours.

It's just one illustration of just how much, true to their original ambition, Candoco have been accepted into the rigorous contemporary dance world. Not only are they seen everywhere from Sadler's Wells to galleries and festivals, they have been repeatedly celebrated on film. In 2012, they performed on possibly the largest stage in the world, at the Paralympic Games' opening and closing ceremonies, watched by millions – something that surely would have been unthinkable back when Celeste and Adam brought the company together.

In 2018, blazing a trail into a whole different world, the company performed on BBC One's *Strictly Come Dancing* in a group performance with the show's professionals. I have to admit, when I heard they were going to be on the programme, I felt a tiny bit smug because of my previous experience with them. (Call it 'I knew them before they were famous...' syndrome.) But regardless of that, what an amazing performance. It was a group dance to David Bowie's *Life on Mars*, and it was just so glamorous and cool and captivating in every way. Watching it, there's a fabulous sense of style in motion – just as you're caught up in the sophisticated elegance, a wheelchair goes spinning past, and then your eye is caught by two dancers who entwine together so seamlessly it takes a moment to realise that a limb is missing. There's an intensity to it that suggests even the seasoned *Strictly* professionals are bringing more than their A game, focused on a real meeting of minds, thinking of the dance in a whole new way. It's just a magical display.

Candoco's appearance on *Strictly* was a testament to how far the perception of integrated dance has come. Being in the industry I am, I know full well the power of that show to change lives, and change opinions, but Charlotte admits that her reaction to it took her by surprise. In the run-up, she approached it as just another process of rehearsal and performance. She knew they were in good hands with choreographer Arlene Phillips, who they had collaborated with before, and she was thinking of it as just another supportive, positive rehearsal experience, the kind of thing that is normal for a hugely experienced dance company that is used to collaborative pieces.

And yet, she says, when it came to the night itself, 'There was something about it just going live on camera, and suddenly knowing that 10 million people, who may not have seen contemporary dance before, who hadn't seen mixed couples before – it was one of the first times that male couples and female couples danced together – and then the whole disabled and non-disabled dancers... I just burst into tears... it took my breath away for a moment.' The realisation of what that moment meant, of how far Candoco had come from a landscape where a leading dance critic would 'prefer not to look', was just extraordinary.

But Charlotte has caught that feeling more than once over the years – not just on a big stage like *Strictly* or the Paralympics. She thinks back to the first time that a proper 1,000-seater theatre audience rose to their feet in a standing ovation, or the breakthroughs they feel today when they tour a country where there is still a lack of understanding of disabled needs. She feels it sometimes in small moments in the studio, when an encounter between two dancers will sometimes come together perfectly, or when a new movement flowers into the space. It gives me spine tingles (and not a little pang of jealousy) just to think about that creative process.

★

Wherever they go in the world, Candoco do more than simply perform. Education is a huge part of their programme, both in the training of dancers and the wider conversation. As Charlotte puts it, 'We try to create really meaningful connections with the audiences, we try to share our profile and our position and our resources to offer opportunities for others, so it proliferates.'

A statement like that is just one of many ways in which Candoco are absolutely the embodiment of what I mean by trailblazing heroes. This, for instance, is how Charlotte describes the ethos of the company: 'I think the point of Candoco is to look at the edge of what we don't know. It has a real pioneering spirit, a real sense of discovery, so there's always a sense of us taking our experience and expertise and skills into a space. We create conditions where risk is possible, and we discover what the possibilities are.'

I love that – creating conditions where risk is possible, and exploring where those possibilities lead: I couldn't ask for a better description of what it means to be a trailblazer.

And as I talk to Charlotte, I realise there is something else in the story, the true measure of their success as trailblazers: where once they stood alone as pioneers in their field, the work they have done over the last 30 years or so means that a whole host of other companies has sprung up alongside them. 'I think largely to do with our international reach and the fact we did residencies and learning workshops and artist development wherever we went, there are now integrated companies all over the world. It's not a new thing,' says Charlotte. Nowadays, 'we are no longer isolated, and we're no longer at the forefront.' Candoco are now part of a constantly evolving international network – perhaps the ultimate mark of success for anyone who is a pioneer.

But with conversations comes challenges, and I am fascinated to hear that, as far as Candoco have come, Charlotte believes there is further to travel. Specifically, the company is realising more and more that in their eagerness at the beginning to be considered on a par with the mainstream contemporary dance companies, they unwittingly modelled their structures and ambitions on what might now be called a normative or traditional model. The time has come, they believe, to challenge this. In particular, they are looking at their behind-the-scenes structures: while the performers onstage are a balanced mixture of disabled and non-disabled artists, this hasn't always been true of the staff body and the choreographers. That is the next step.

It's a journey that I think is being played out in all sorts of progressive organisations – you start out with the best of intentions and achieve a shift in the culture, but that very shift in turn challenges your own preconceived ideas. Characteristically, Charlotte and the company are embracing this shift with real excitement, even if it is a daunting one at times. Specifically, Charlotte would love to share the leadership role once again with a disabled peer, as she has done before. 'There's a lot to learn,' she says, which is a wonderful statement from someone who has been learning and teaching for so many years.

However far they have come, and however much they have transformed the possibilities for disabled dancers, Candoco feel there is so much further to go. Charlotte dreams of expanding the number of disabled teachers in this country; at the moment there simply aren't enough: 'We are still failing so many disabled artists through our traditional approaches to training, they are still so exclusive,' she says, and is looking for ways to transform this. She wants increased representation, not just of disabled artists but other underrepresented groups. 'More, better, wider' is how she describes it, and she believes that we are on the brink of further exciting change, if only we can harness genuine equitable opportunity.

It has been more than a pleasure, all these years later, to connect with Charlotte and delve back into the world of Candoco. There's a part of me that would love to don the leotard and tights again and get down to the studio. But at a more significant level, I'm just so in awe of what they have done. I think about the individual lives they must have touched – audience members who have seen something that has expanded their intellectual and aesthetic horizons; television viewers who have had their eyes and minds opened just that little bit wider through watching them dance; people who have caught a performance of theirs and realised possibilities that never felt open to them before; people with bodies that are different who see themselves reflected in a way they never had imagined... Candoco have been changing the conversation about what it means to be differently abled for more than 30 years, and they are still finding new and wonderful avenues to explore. More than just a dance company, they have the power to move, in every possible way.

Craig Jones

Imagine a man who loves his job – who has dreamed of doing it since he was a boy and who started in his chosen field as early as he possibly could. Who has risen up to positions of great responsibility and achievement, and whose career is as meaningful as it can possibly be. Who has a bright future ahead of him in an organisation that is more than just a workplace, it's a way of life. Now imagine that every day, that man – or woman – lives in fear that one fundamental and perfectly legal aspect of themselves will be discovered. And that if it is they will be ruined: not just sacked but disgraced and possibly jailed. That was the position that Craig Jones was in, only 25 years ago. His career? He was serving in the Royal Navy. His secret? That he was gay.

Sometimes the trailblazing heroes that I have met for this book serve as a reminder of how different the world was just a few short years ago. But I have to say that meeting Craig was a jolt, because the world he describes is one that, I am glad to say, seems extraordinarily foreign now. Nowadays, the landscape of the armed forces is entirely transformed in this regard, not least because of the trail that Craig himself blazed.

★

For Craig, love for the Royal Navy had been embedded in him his whole life. He had an uncle who had been in the navy after the Second World War, and since he had been a boy nothing excited him more than the idea of joining. The walls of his boyhood rooms were plastered with pictures of frigates and destroyers, and as soon as he could, at the age of 17, he spent a 'really frightening' three days at an interview with the imposing Admiralty Interview Board. It was not a success: 'Mr Jones, thank you for your interest, but we don't think you'll make a good naval officer now or at any time in the future' was the response. (He admits that they were probably right – he was too young and inexperienced at the time.) But Craig is clearly a determined soul, and after a couple of years at university in Portsmouth (handily close to the Royal Naval base), he tried again, and was accepted. You can imagine how exciting this must have felt – a real dream-come-true moment at the prospect of training at the Britannia Royal Naval college. The then 20-year-old Craig must have felt that his bright future was assured. And in a way, it was.

That was, until a 'moment of epiphany' happened just as he finished his university finals, two months before he was due to start his training. Walking past a newsagent's, he bought a copy of the *Radio Times*. Taking it back to his rooms, he sat down on his bed – surrounded of course by posters of naval ships on the walls – 'And I thought, "Oh my crikey, I've bought that because it's got a picture of Michael Ball on the front."'

Talking about it now, you can tell that Craig still has an almost cinematic recall of the dominoes that fell into place in his brain at that moment: 'I thought, "Oh no, I fancy Michael Ball. I must be gay."' Swiftly followed, of course, by the realisation that this was something that did not fit in the slightest with his desire to be a naval officer. He can tell the story now with every detail clear: his position on the bed, the moment he said out loud, but in a whisper – 'I'm gay' – fearful just in case somebody somehow would hear it through the closed door. He tells the story with a laugh, but it's a rueful one, and it doesn't mask how seismic this realisation must have been.

This was the late 1980s, so positive role models for LGBT+ people were in pretty short supply and coming out still wasn't easy for most people. But for Craig there was much more than the usual fear. He was about to join – he longed to join – an organisation in which his sexual orientation, though perfectly legal in society at large, was expressly forbidden. Which meant that he had to make a conscious decision 'to leave my sexual orientation at the main gate'. Which is a pretty big choice for a young man of 21 to have to make.

In every other respect, all Craig's hopes were to come true over the coming years. After basic training he was sent out to the Caribbean: he describes it as the *Boy's Own* adventure of his dreams, working as an armed boarding officer with the US Coastguard to intercept cocaine trading vessels. After that he retrained as a helicopter fast-drop insertion officer. (This is as terrifying and seriously cool as it sounds – it's the people who shimmy down ropes out of helicopters...) This training took him out to the first Gulf War in 1991, after which he became a patrol officer in South Down during the Troubles in

Northern Ireland. Everything he did, he says, 'really lit me up.' He was doing work that was meaningful, he was having all the excitement and adventure you could imagine. But there was a large part of his life that was simply missing. As far as he was concerned, that was just the way it had to be.

The events that would change his life came in two stages. It was 1994 and he was still serving in Northern Ireland. He was out on a naval patrol with an officer from the RUC, and seeing a small fishing vessel they hailed it, only to get no response. The next step was to board the vessel; still no one on deck. The officer 'rather bravely' suggested to him that he might like to go first down the hatch, so he went over – in full bulky body armour – and looked down. What he saw there was a scene that he was not prepared for: two young men lying in each other's arms. You get the sense that he was caught off guard himself by his reaction to this: 'I was profoundly shocked. But also instinctively protective.' He knew full well that what they were doing was hugely risky for them. It wasn't just that the age of consent at the time was 21: this was Northern Ireland, not a place where it was easy to be gay. So what those two young men were doing 'took some degree of courage', courage that Craig realised he didn't yet have. Not wanting the RUC officer behind him to see them, he pretended to get his bulky body suit stuck in the hatch, and allowed them to get themselves dressed and in order before they came up on deck for some routine questioning.

Once he was back on his ship, he felt shamed by the courage of those two young men, and shattered by the realisation that unlike them he was denying something huge and true about himself. It was this moment that led to the next huge step he took – six weeks later, having completed his tour in Northern Ireland, he went back to the UK and walked into the first gay bar he had ever been in.

Now, I imagine any young man walking into his first gay bar – especially if he has waited until the age of 25 to do so – is approaching those doors with a mixture of huge excitement and adrenaline but also trepidation. But mixed in with that for Craig was a real, and very well-founded fear. To understand why, you need to understand the culture – and the law – of the navy in the 1990s. Never mind the fact that being gay had been legal in society since 1967. In the navy, stepping into that gay bar meant that Craig was opening himself up to a life of 'looking over my shoulder for the day when the Royal Military Police would catch me.' If he had been caught, the events that would have followed sound simply barbaric: 'I would have been arrested, taken away for questioning by the Royal Military Police Special Investigation Branch. That often lasted for three or four days. I would have been sent to a military hospital for a medical inspection that had no place alongside the Hippocratic Oath. Then I would have been court-martialled, I would have been given a six-month prison sentence, I would have had my medals… ceremonially ripped from my uniform, and I would have been dismissed in disgrace.'

None of this was theoretical. It happened, but in a shrouded, shadowy way that made it even more sinister: 'It was a completely toxic subject. You would leave the ship on a Friday, come back on a Monday, and somebody would be missing.' To ask too many questions was to invite speculation as to why you were so interested. If you tried to stay in contact with people who had disappeared after they had gone, well, 'What's that all about? Is there something about you?' The last thing anyone wanted to do was to invite the military police to their own door. If anyone had known Craig's secret they were beholden to report it. There were people in prison – both military detention quarters and civilian prisons – for this 'offence'.

I repeat: this was 1994. Homosexuality was completely legal in society, the very society that the navy was sworn to protect. I must admit – and I know this makes me sound naïve – that the culture Craig is describing is so foreign to me that I find it really hard to process. Remember – I was a dance student at the time, as you've already read, spending my days rolling round a studio floor in leggings. In my world, people's sexuality by this point in time was neither here nor there. The idea that somebody would be treated like this purely on the basis of being gay is like something from another era. It brings me up sharply, the realisation of quite what a bubble I was able to live in. And the challenges faced by those like Craig who didn't have that luxury.

★

He would spend the next period of his life 'looking round corners'. Up until this point, his sexuality had been a secret, but one that was easy enough to keep because apart from his carefully suppressed thoughts, he had nothing to hide. But in that very first gay bar, on that very first night, Craig met the man who was to become his husband of 28 years and counting. 'And if that doesn't bring military efficiency to dating, I don't know what does,' says Craig – a brilliant line, and he's certainly got a point!

So he and Adam had a heady, hidden romance. 'Life in

technicolour,' says Craig, adding that it's never a good idea to have your very first relationship at 25. It was intense, fast and clearly wonderful: in fact, in just a short time Craig started living with Adam and his parents, who lived near Portsmouth and were wonderfully welcoming. (He invented a convenient uncle and aunt to explain this to his colleagues.)

Professionally, Craig had just landed the job of his dreams, as navigator of the frigate HMS *Sheffield*. (Even now, you can feel the wistful excitement about the role come across in Craig's voice: 'I love driving ships. I wish I could go back and do it again.') But the two parts of his life were irreconcilable, and the tension was becoming too much. When Adam's father died very suddenly, just two months before the *Sheffield* was due to leave on exercise, everything came to the boil. With his lover's family in crisis, there was no support at all available to Craig. In any other circumstances he would have been enveloped by the protection of the navy (he cites the armed forces covenant that 'those who stand in the nation's need, in their own moment of need will be supported'). Needless to say, there could be no question of support for him.

When the *Sheffield* sailed, Craig was on it as navigator. But it was less than 24 hours before he was evacuated off it by helicopter, 'in a bit of a mess really'. Coping with the conflicting demands in his life had simply become too much. After an encounter with an army psychiatrist who more or less told him to go home and get some rest, Craig was given two months off before resuming his duties. The hollow 'victory' was that he had managed to avoid revealing his secret. But of course, in the naval culture of the time, this was an episode that was not exactly beneficial to his career.

The next years were strange ones for Craig. The dichotomy at the heart of his existence meant that though on the surface he participated in naval life just as he should, a part of himself was dislocated. You can sense his deep love for the camaraderie and bonds of the navy jostling with the anger he was beginning to feel when he describes that time: 'People in the armed forces share a great deal about themselves. When we go away to operations or conflict or disaster relief for months and months at a time there is a moment when you sit in the bar and share everything.' But of course, Craig had to hold back. If you had met him then, he says, you would have seen him as somebody who didn't 100 per cent take part. He had to arrange his life in a way that was fundamentally deceptive. He and Adam lived in Brighton, for instance, far away from any naval bases. Being seen pushing a trolley round the supermarket together at the weekend could have brought disaster.

A burning sense of injustice began to grow – a realisation that the armed forces that he continued to love so much had an enormous blind spot. That the very people who were sworn to protect the values of a free society were being denied those freedoms themselves.

One particular incident summed up the grotesque compromises Craig was being forced to make, when an open letter was printed in the *Daily Mail* in which the then First Sea Lord said he hoped he 'never had to serve with queers and lesbians'. Reading this on board the carrier HMS *Illustrious* with some fellow officers, Craig had what he calls now his 'moment of Judas': 'I hope I never have to serve with them too,' he said. You get the sense even now that he finds it hard to forgive himself that moment. From then on, he swore, while he still could not be truthful, he would at least be 'grey' on the subject.

By now, it was 1996, a time when the debate about the armed forces ban was beginning to hot up throughout the military, and across wider society. LGBTQ+ charity Stonewall was bringing cases from disgraced servicemen and women Robert Ely, Jeanette Smith, Duncan Lustig Prean, Graham Grady and John Beckett to the highest courts in the land and beyond. The topic was coming up again and again in mess halls and military banquets. Craig began to find his voice a little on the subject, starting with a grand lunch he had been invited to by Admiral Roy Clare, the captain of an aircraft carrier. As the most junior officer at the table (everyone else was a commodore), he kept his counsel as the senior officers aired their views. But when Admiral Clare turned to him to ask his opinion, he found for the first time the courage to offer at least some honesty – that 'gay men have served in the military for over 500 years. That they have been doing a damn good job, and the sooner we accept their presence and recognise that they are part of why we are some of the best armed forces in the world, then we will be a lot better off.'

The reaction? 'Tumbleweed,' says Craig now, laughing. He was rescued by Admiral Clare, who said something that must have been like oil on troubled waters for Craig. He agreed, and further, he said something that Craig still remembers to this day: 'The values of the ban are not the values of the armed forces I joined.'

★

The ban on homosexuals in the armed forces was lifted on 12th January 2000. It is perhaps fair to say that the military had been dragged to this kicking and screaming: it came as a result of a European Court of Human Rights ruling on a case brought to them by Stonewall. In other words, the ban, quite simply, was illegal, and would have to be overturned. Reactionary politicians and commentators acceded to this grudgingly – Geoff Hoon, then Secretary of State for Defence, commented that 'we cannot choose the decisions we implement. The status quo is simply not an option… the law is the law.' While he might have finished up the statement with 'I have no doubt this is the best way forward', it was hardly a ringing endorsement, and his insistence also that sexuality should be a 'private matter' pointed to a desire that gay people should basically keep quiet.

Keeping quiet was not something Craig was prepared to do. He came out on the day the ban was lifted. The next phase of his life – the trailblazing phase that was to have such an impact – was about to begin. As head of operations on the flagship on which he was serving, part of his job was to take the signals to his commanding officer. When the announcement came through on 11th January – still under embargo – Craig was therefore one of the first people to learn about it. The reaction of the commanding officer was disheartening, to say the least. As was the discussion the next day when the other officers were mustered and told of the ruling. Once again 'some of the comment in the room was exceptionally negative'. Craig could be silent no longer. 'Remember, officers lead people,' he says: these were the people who were about to announce the ruling to the 500-strong crew. He simply couldn't bear the briefing to the whole ship to be given in the same style that he had just heard from his fellow officers so he followed the captain to his cabin, and said, 'You need to know this.'

Craig is exceptionally frank and detailed as he tells his story, but I suspect that this conversation is something he prefers not to have to think about in detail. 'It was a very sombre and difficult conversation,' he says, 'but I have never regretted it.'

Craig, as a lieutenant commander at the time was the highest-ranking member of the navy to come out. The importance of him doing so cannot be overestimated. The ban might have gone, but the culture of an organisation, especially an organisation like the navy, doesn't change in a heartbeat. It is driven by the actions and the attitudes of the people within it. Which is why it was such a significant thing for Craig to come out when he did. 'I came out into a toxic situation,' he said. For months, conversations stopped when he walked into a room. 'There were officers in my ship who wouldn't go into the same shower block as me for a period of months.' And there were almost surreal moments of humour, too – like the fuss about what should happen about the formal Burns Night supper that was taking place only two weeks after the ban had been lifted. Craig was pulled aside by both the captain and his second-in-command to ask if he was intending to dance with Adam that night. 'Well, it's a ceilidh, so I imagine that we'll all probably dance, but if you think I'm going to be gliding round the ballroom in his arms, it seems unlikely,' was his answer. In the event, once Adam had bravely donned his black tie and ventured into the lion's den, Craig never got the chance: Adam was too busy dancing with the officers' wives.

Gradually during this time, he began to feel the attitudes towards him on board the ship soften. There were those who had stood by him from the outset, and slowly, as people began to see him for who he was, the hushed whispers around him seemed to stop.

★

The next years of Craig's life became focused on campaigning within the navy: 'What became important was supporting the armed forces to be brilliant employers of LGBT+ people.' The ban might have been lifted, but they were a million miles away from that. As it stood, support for gay people in the service was basically non-existent: 'There were no ameliorating measures, there were no education programmes, no training, no effort to protect people.'

Craig saw that he was in a particularly important position: he was a senior enough officer with enough experience that he was unlikely to bear the brunt of any serious bullying. But he knew that thousands of other servicemen and women were not so fortunate. He owed it to them to try and change things.

He started off by writing – completely against regulations – 'lots and lots of angry letters to admirals and generals and air marshals and to the Secretary of State.' He spoke up whenever he could – once at a naval 'diversity conference' in Portsmouth where the top brass had gathered to show off all the policies it had in place – 'for race and faith and ethnicity and women and disability and social mobility'. But in spite of the fact that the ban had by this time been lifted for several years, the topic of gay rights still didn't arise. When the opportunity for audience questions came up, Craig leapt up and said to the Second Sea Lord, 'Sir, I've listened to you talk about every protected characteristic you can imagine, but despite the fact we've been persecuting LGBT people for 40 years you still dare not speak their name.'

None of this, sadly, gained much traction. He was told off for sending letters against protocol. As for his outburst at the conference, it didn't go down well.

'But you never know when your moment of luck is coming,' says Craig now. A couple of days later he and Adam were attending the Trooping the Colour, and found themselves sitting next to a smart-looking older gentleman. 'How has your week been?' said the man. When Craig said honestly, 'Well you know, sir, it has been absolutely appalling,' his ears pricked up, and he asked why. As the parade marched by, the man invited him to tell him more ('I've seen this ceremonial stuff about 25 times, I'm sure your story's more interesting,' he said), and gave Craig the opportunity to talk about his crusade. That man turned out to be Baron Armstrong of Ilminster, a highly ranked civil servant who had been Cabinet Secretary in previous years, and who was extraordinarily well connected. By the time Craig had finished putting his case, he was offering to help.

That help started with an invitation to spend a weekend at Leeds Castle, where he was a trustee. One of the other guests was the First Sea Lord, Admiral Lord West of Spithead. Finally, Craig had the ear of somebody right at the top. He was able to explain why this was a moment in history where the Royal Navy had a chance to lead the way, to free its servicemen and women to work at their full potential without fear of stigma, and to make a real difference.

'He got it, absolutely got it,' says Craig now.

★

Some weeks later, the Royal Navy became the first armed force in the world to march in uniform at Pride. It made headlines round the world – in no small part down to Craig, who rang up every journalist he could think of in Fleet Street. This was in the teeth of the other armed services, who were allowing their men and women to march, but only in polo shirts. ('The Royal Navy will never march in polo shirts through the streets of our capital city,' said Admiral Lord West.) It was a sign of the change that was to come. The Royal Navy joined Stonewall as diversity champions. There are now networks and support groups for LGBT+ servicepeople. Gay men and women are allowed to get married on their ships, the navy advertises for employees in gay magazines, and recruits at Pride events. On the twentieth anniversary of the lifting of the ban, naval bases flew rainbow flags, and the naval base in Portsmouth was lit up in rainbow colours. Today, someone like Craig joining the Royal Navy would have no need to try and cauterise a whole part of their being. They would have no fear of the Royal Military Police laying a hand on their shoulder. They wouldn't have to change their friends' names in their address book in case someone might catch sight of it and wonder why male names were paired in there. They would be free to get on with being the best servicemen and women they could possibly be. It is an extraordinary transformation.

Craig left the navy in 2008, and became head of diversity at Barclays Bank. But his crusade was not entirely finished: while things have changed for today's LGBT+ men and women in the forces, there was still no redress for those who suffered –

disgraced, dismissed and sometimes even jailed before the ban was lifted. Craig came together with some of these veterans to form Fighting with Pride, which seeks to gain recognition and restoration of medals for all those that suffered most during that time.

What strikes me strongly when talking to Craig is that his deep love for the navy – formed back in that childhood bedroom with its pictures of battleships on the wall – is still as strong today as it ever was. It is clearly written into every fibre of his being. This is a man who talks with such pride and admiration for the band of brothers and sisters he knows the navy to be. He embodies all the virtues of the service – courage, determination, a quiet decency. He knows what it means to stand up in the service of your country, and has thought more than most about the values he was sworn to defend.

It must have been soul-wrenching that for so long his very existence ran counter to the institution he loves. But it's thanks to his determination and courage that nobody will have to go through the same thing he did: the definition of the difference a true trailblazer can make.

community heroes

The RNLI

Port Isaac, Cornwall. It's one of my favourite places in the world, a tiny little harbour village on the north coast of the county. If you were asked to imagine the perfect Cornish fishing village, this would be the place you would conjure. Brightly coloured fishermen's boats bob in the harbour, there are crab pots everywhere, seagulls crow, and little slate-covered buildings line ridiculously narrow streets that tumble down the hill to the crescent of the sea – beautifully turquoise at the height of summer, wonderfully stormy when the weather is up.

I've been coming down here since I was a boy – my uncle comes from here, and my Auntie Jan is a stalwart of the place, teaching at the school and playing the organ in the local church, St Endellion. For me, it is a place that feels like family: my mum and dad had a house here throughout my childhood, and so did another set of my cousins, so in the holidays we would spend as much time there as we could, and sometimes at Christmas there would be 30 of us round the kitchen table, laughing and shouting and interrupting each other. Christmas is a particularly magical time in the village – smoke drifts from the chimneys so you can smell the log fires in the cold air as you walk to the couple of pubs that form the hub of the village social life. It's a place where everyone knows everyone else and, right at the heart of the community, its always-open doors facing out into the crescent of the bay, stands a simple boathouse. In white letters on a navy-blue background, English on top, and Cornish underneath, the sign reads: Port Isaac Lifeboat Station. The sign's emblem is a white flag with a red cross and the initials RNLI. Four letters that spell out a long and extraordinary tradition of everyday heroism.

The Port Isaac station is not a particularly amazing building – just a medium-sized boatshed. It houses (for the moment at least, they are planning a move) the training room and general office, which is a busy, slightly cluttered space, walls filled with pictures and shelves, and desks crowded with computers. A door off the office leads into the heart of the lifeboat station itself. Here there is definite order. Each piece of equipment has its place: in cupboards on the walls hang ranks of yellow drysuits and grey 'bunny suits' – the glorified onesies to wear underneath – each one named and carefully hung up, waiting for the next time they are needed. Shelves in alcoves house ranks of white helmets and orange lifejackets. The centrepiece of the station, next to the tractor that will help launch it, is, of course, the lifeboat itself. This is the *Copeland Bell*, a D-class, 16ft boat with a 50cc horsepower engine on the back. This relatively simple type of boat is not too expensive – at £50,000 it is one of the cheaper boats in the fleet – but it is responsible for over 60 per cent of all the work done by the

RNLI. It's reliable, practical and can get into almost any sea: it's a workhorse.

And what work that is. Even if we don't live by the coast ourselves, I think most of us have a warm feeling towards the RNLI. Perhaps we have stepped into one of their lifeboat stations on holiday, and bought a badge or a toy boat as a souvenir. We might have bought their Christmas cards. We might have taken our children to look at the lifeboat and chat to the friendly crew. But what we might not consider is just how the ordinary men and women of the RNLI are routinely putting themselves in harm's way to save lives. The RNLI undertakes an average of 24 launches every day, aiding thousands at risk on the sea, and saving hundreds of lives a year. They are on call 24 hours a day, 365 days a year. All of this without government funding: it is a charity and the men and women who put out to sea are largely volunteers.

If you've ever been nearby when an RNLI shout goes off, you'll know the drama of it. Up until a few years ago, they used to summon the crew at Port Isaac by maroons – rockets which they would send up when the crew was needed. One rocket for the coastguard, two rockets for the RNLI, three for both. If you were in the village and heard the first rocket go off, you would wait on tenterhooks for the second, and then there would be a mad dash down to the Platt – the flat area in front of the harbour – to watch the boat being launched. Nowadays, there is slightly less drama – they use pagers instead of the rockets – but the village is so small that everyone seems to know pretty quickly when something is afoot. Before that pager goes off the members of the crew – there are about 18 seagoing crew and eight shore crew at the moment, in 2022 – are just ordinary people doing ordinary things. They are farmers, builders, fish merchants, painters and decorators, businessmen and women: all manner of things in their daily lives. Nicky Bradbury, one of the stalwarts of the crew, runs the local bakery, Nicky B's: if you're in Port Isaac, she's the person to go to for a pasty. But the second that pager goes off, she and the others will race towards the station, and within four minutes they are in drysuits ready to head into whatever the shout requires. The sign above the door between the rooms in the station states one simple maxim: 'Rush Slowly', and the crew take that adage seriously, because they are being called for a purpose, and that purpose is to go and help someone in trouble, no matter what that trouble may be.

The first three of the correct rank to reach the station man the lifeboat. The next three launch it. There's a huge rush of adrenaline even watching the shout in progress: the carefully choreographed ballet of the men and women intent on their task, the moment when they start the engine, the sight of the little orange boat leaving the bay and heading into whatever is required.

But the romance and excitement of it all mask the fact that this is serious and often very dangerous work. As the boat disappears from view, the spectators on land have no idea what they are heading for. Even the crew have no way of knowing exactly what they will be facing, and on what seas. To launch the boat, a process has to be gone through – the launch authority at Falmouth ring through to make sure that the conditions are acceptable. That decision is the responsibility of an individual who doesn't go out to sea himself, the Deputy Launching Authority (DLA): it's a kind of safety net. Nevertheless, the sea is always unpredictable: 'We launch from here with a very detailed brief, and by the time we've got two miles across the bay it's changed. That's the nature of nature. The tide's come in, the surf's increased, the tide's gone out, the surf's dropped off... whichever way it can swing and change as you make your way across the bay,' says Damien Bolton, senior helmsman at the station.

Port Isaac is a beautiful place, but it is remote, and that remoteness means that it can be unforgiving: the nearest all-weather lifeboat station is 25 minutes away by sea from the harbour, and if the boat is at the extremities of the Port Isaac patch it could take them up to 55 minutes before another boat can come to assist them. Coastguard 924, the helicopter which runs from Newquay Airport, can be on the scene within ten minutes of launch, but the crew know that, essentially, they have to rely on themselves. The nature of the work means they are trained to go and do the absolute opposite of what other boats do; they need to go towards trouble. The kit and the training programmes the RNLI has developed are second to none, but at the end of the day accidents do happen.

'Where other people would be saying, "Don't put a boat in there, don't do that, don't do this," in the end we say, "Well, we *have* to go in there, we *have* to do that, we *have* to do this,"' says Damien. The shout might turn out to be anything from a teenager who has been blown out to sea on an inflatable unicorn – a comical rescue that in the right conditions is pretty straightforward – to the most tragic or dramatic of situations. Whatever it is, the crew have to be prepared to meet all circumstances.

★

I'm proud to say that Damien is a friend of mine. I've known him since we were both teenagers. His family came from this area, but he himself was brought up in Berkshire, and it wasn't until he was 15, in 1995, that they moved back. My Auntie Jan always had a Boxing Day drinks party at her house, which was a mainstay of Christmas, and the whole village would come. That was where I first met Damien and his elder brothers, and from that moment onwards my siblings and cousins and I had three more friends to go to the pub with. (Damien was technically too young for that, but nobody seemed to mind him being there – he was already taller than me, even though I was two years older.)

Damien was always destined to be part of the village, even before his family moved back. It's in his DNA – cut him open and you'd see the words Port Isaac running through him. Even as a small child, he had spent enough time in Port Isaac to be thoroughly captured by the romance of the place and of the RNLI itself. One of his early memories is of holding his mother's hand as he looked at the lifeboat: 'Mum, I'm going to be on that boat one day,' he said.

His mother took a practical view: 'Well, Damien, you probably won't be 'cause we live in Cookham and they don't have a lifeboat in Cookham.' It turns out, though, that Damien was right and his mum was wrong. Within a year of moving to the area, when he was still 16 ('officially 17') Damien joined the lifeboat crew. In truth, it was a family affair: on the same day, his dad joined the Coastguard and his mum joined the RNLI committee.

Damien's first year encapsulated the range of situations that the lifeboat crew finds itself in. His very first shout was a pretty standard rescue: a fisherman on the rocks cut off from the tide on a fairly calm day. That's a pretty simple operation: the crew goes and gets them off the rocks and delivers them to safety, and this being Damien's first ever rescue he fulfilled the time-honoured tradition of buying everybody back at the station a beer.

His second shout, though, summed up the harsher realities that come with being in the service: it was the suicide of a girl who had jumped off the cliff at a neighbouring beach, jumping 300ft and landing on the flat rocks at the bottom. As one of three men in the boat, at the age of 17, dealing with the consequences of what he had to do on that day was a tough call: 'In those days we dealt with it the way we used to, in the pub, a few beers, a few chats. Obviously not the best way of dealing with something like that...' It was when the local newspaper came out that the tragic reality of what he had seen really hit home for Damien: the front page carried the girl's picture and an article about her. It made the human side of what he had witnessed horribly real. For the next year, every time he walked back to his farm late at night after a darts game at the pub, he could see the lights in the distance from the local youth hostel near where she had jumped. He found himself haunted by the image; he would take off his shoes and walk along slapping the soles together; a warding-off, perhaps, as well as a tribute.

Damien has been a part of the RNLI crew ever since, eventually becoming a senior helmsman. There is a huge responsibility on the shoulders of a helmsman: on each boat that goes out they have ultimate responsibility for the decisions made. They have to have exceptional skills and seamanship, of course, but above all they need to have the implicit trust of the crew. And the helmsman has to trust himself to take on responsibility not just for the people they are rescuing, but for the crew as well: 'A conscious thought every time I go to sea or run a training session with the guys is that we are being gifted the responsibility by a loved one to take a loved one out to sea, whether father, brother, sister or mother, whoever it is. And I have a responsibility to return them safely to the station.'

In Damien's own home, next to the telly, is a radio scanner. When he goes out to sea his three young daughters gather round it as though it is an open fire, listening to what their father is doing, and when he gets back they are togged up in their wellies and hats playing lifeboats. There's a huge amount of pride in knowing his daughters feel the romance of the sea themselves, but there is a flip side as well. There are times when his wife Amy has to turn off the scanner, distracting the girls from what their father is doing out on the waves because of the danger of what he is facing.

One particular rescue by the Port Isaac team brought this sense of responsibility into stark reality – the April morning in 2012 when he and Nicky Bradbury and Matt Main launched the boat in response to reports that two men had been seen in the water near the cliffs at Tregardock. It was a high tide with a three-metre swell, and the wind was nearing Force Five and blowing onshore, which meant that when they reached the scene seven minutes later, the waves were hitting the cliffs hard and bouncing back off them, and the water was churning and deadly. They knew there were two individuals who had been in the water for about half an hour, swept off the rocks while fishing, but all they could see was one man being tumbled among the waves, hemmed in by a crescent of semi-submerged rocks. He managed to raise his arm and call out to the lifeboat once before being swept under again. It was immediately clear that the first challenge was to get the boat anywhere near the two men. Calling on all his experience and seamanship, Damien used a technique called 'veering down', using an anchor line to tether the boat and then paying it out to reverse towards the figures in the sea, while the waves battered them from all sides. They managed to get within shouting distance – two metres – of the men, and three metres off the cliffs. But Damien spotted a rope – it turned out to be from the lifebuoy with which they had tried to rescue themselves – and knew that if they got any closer it was going to get tangled up in the boat's propeller. Worse, only one of the men had shown any sign of consciousness. This was Paul Sleeman, who was 27 at the time. The other man in the sea, ominously still, was his father, Peter. Paul was desperately trying to hold onto his inert body; the effort he had clearly expended in clinging onto his fully clothed father in the heaving waves must have been immense.

The crew called to Paul to swim towards the boat, knowing that to do so he would have to do the unthinkable and let go of his father. He refused, and at this point Damien had to call on all his reserves of authority and order the drowning man to let go and swim to safety. Paul surrendered, swam those two metres, and as he reached the side, sank into unconsciousness. It took all the crew's strength to haul him aboard. As they did so, they realised that he had tied himself to his father. To get him on the boat, they had to cut Peter free and re-tie the rope to the lifeboat. It was at this point that a huge wave crashed over them, knocking out the engine as Paul slipped in and out of consciousness. Luckily the sturdy workhorse that is the D-class boat came to their rescue: the restart button worked, and the engines flared back to life.

With Paul's life clearly hanging in the balance from hypothermia and the risk of secondary drowning, and the threat of the boat being overturned still present, they cut the anchor line that was tethering them and as soon as they had the engine back, they cleared themselves of the rocks and cliffs, still towing Peter's body behind them. It was only once they were safe from the immediate danger that they could pull Peter alongside and check for signs of life: there were none. The focus now became the ever-worsening condition that Paul was in, and it became clear that to save him, they were going to have to cut his father's body loose and come back to collect it later. Damien fitted a lifejacket to the body so that they could come back to recover it as soon as possible, and made the heartrending decision to cut him loose. Nicky and Matt administered first aid to the failing Paul as Damien called for an immediate evacuation. The relief as the search-and-rescue helicopter appeared moments later must have been phenomenal, the knowledge that Paul was being airlifted to the best possible care tempered by the necessity of going back to retrieve his father's body. The crew knew just how important it would be to the family to have their loved one returned to them for burial: 'To be able to return something so precious to other people so that they have some closure is amazing,' says Damien.

Damien, Nicky and Matt were all awarded honours due to their actions that day – Damien received the RNLI Silver medal for gallantry, and both Nicky and Matt the Bronze. One of Damien's most prized possessions stems from that time – not an award or a certificate, but a painting done by local artist Katie Childs. It reaches back into the past and depicts the moment when Damien as a child, holding his mother's hand, made a vow to be on that lifeboat one day. But in this painting, it is the adult Damien holding the hand of his younger self: it's a picture that looks back to the past and forward into the future, just as the service itself does.

You get the sense that Damien's pride in the crew's actions that day lies not in any of the recognition that he was given for it, but in the teamwork that the three of them shared; the fact that they put their lives in each other's hands and got on with the job. There was tragedy inextricably mixed in with that rescue, and to take on the role of helmsman means making those tough calls, opening yourself up to the possibility of being haunted by what you did or didn't do. Thinking back to that day now, Damien describes it as 'a double-edged sword': 'On the one hand we brought back a son who was brought back to full fitness and has now got married and had kids and is living a healthy life. But we also brought back his deceased father, who is in the church where they got married, and was laid to rest next to the aisle that they walked down.' Those are the harsh realities of the role.

★

Every time the shout goes up, the crew who hasten to answer it are laying themselves open to the possibility of tragedy. Being one of the spectators watching the boat launch, listening to the stories of daring on the high seas, it's easy to get lost in the romance and the heroism of it all, but there's a lot of emotional trauma that comes with that territory. Every year on 19th December, the RNLI shares out a documentary in remembrance of the Penlee lifeboat disaster, and every year Damien watches it, in recognition of what happened on that date in 1981. It's a sobering reminder: it describes the night when the Penlee lifeboat, the *Solomon Browne*, with its eight volunteer lifeboatmen, went to the assistance of the stricken *Union Star* in horrendous weather. There is a section of that documentary that jerks you straight back to that night. Matter-of-fact, but plainly exhausted, the voice of the captain of the lifeboat comes over the radio after their first run at the rescue: 'Falmouth Coastguard, Falmouth Coastguard. This is Penlee Lifeboat calling Falmouth Coastguard... We've got four men off at the moment, male and female. There's two left on board.' Then there is a jolt, and then silence. When the coastguard answers their call there is nothing but static hiss. And over the airwaves comes the repeated call from land: 'Penlee Lifeboat, Penlee Lifeboat. This is Falmouth Coastguard.' Nothing comes back, no matter how many times the coastguard makes the call. All the crew on that lifeboat were lost that night, along with everyone on the *Union Star*. Those voices, 40 years on, are haunting. It was an appalling tragedy for the community at Penlee, and for the families involved. For a lifeboatman like Damien, it is a reminder of how vulnerable every lifeboat crew is up and down the country, and what the potential cost of his calling can be.

But for Damien and the rest of the crew, the dangers are worth it. The walls of the lifeboat station at Port Isaac are pictures of people and families who owe their existence to the RNLI. 'We've got letters round the station that have been sent to us over the years, pictures of families and existences that wouldn't be there if it wasn't for something that some of us at the station did. It's amazing to think that there's the pitter patter of tiny feet [because of us],' says Damien.

Recently he was given the honour of making a speech at one of the St Endellion music festivals. St Endellion is the beautiful local church where, as I said, my Auntie Jan plays the organ. It's close to my heart as many of my family have got married there, and every year it hosts a fantastic festival, at which there is a 'Thought for the Day', delivered by a notable person. In 2021, Damien was given this honour, and he chose for his subject the word 'custodian', because in his view that is at the heart of the service. The members of the RNLI crew are there to be custodians for people at some of the most horrific points in their lives, when they are at their most vulnerable or most scared. To be charged with this custodianship is an honour that he doesn't take lightly.

Talking to Damien reinforces the very special place the RNLI occupies at the heart of the Port Isaac community. The service doesn't just exist on the water, it exists throughout the DNA of the whole county and the whole coastline. This was something that was really brought home to him over the course of the pandemic: 'The RNLI is over 150 years old, so for the last 150 years there have been three focal points within the village: the lifeboat station, the pub and the church, and all three of those entities were closed.' The doors to the lifeboat station were shut in the daytime for the first time anybody could remember. The only other times those doors are closed is for specific tragedies – when a body is brought back to the station, or the moment in 1998 when the boat was lost in the caves at Bosinney. So the sight of those closed doors, shutting off what was going on inside from the outside world, felt like a scar in the heart of the village. It went on for week after week after week. The crew were still ready and working, but they were closed off from the village itself.

It was a time when the expertise and humanity of the crew were needed more than ever, not just for their seagoing activities but also for their work in the community. The crew are trained as community first responders, so that if an ambulance is more than eight minutes away, they can call on the team to go in and be the first point of contact: to take vital signs, assess the situation, assist until the ambulance arrives. During the pandemic, this aspect of the work came to the fore. Responding one day to a woman who had had a cardiac incident, Damien started to take her blood pressure. When he held her hand to push her sleeve up, she burst into tears. Horrified that he might have hurt her, Damien stopped immediately, but her response shocked him: it turned out that this was the first physical touch she had had from another human in 18 months. Such was the toll the pandemic took on the community, and the shuttering of the lifeboat station was emblematic of everything the community was going through: 'The day it re-opened was amazing,' says Damien.

★

If the RNLI is the heart of the village, that heart relies on fundraising, and it is one way you can tell just how important the service is considered to be by everyone in Port Isaac. It's a huge community effort, one that goes on year after year:

everything from the local women who make and sell preserves on behalf of the charity – Janet Shadbolt's pickled eggs can fetch up to a £100, such is the power of this tradition – to the local restaurant which over the course of six years has probably donated about £50,000. A few years ago, the station needed a new boat: this is given by the central RNLI when it is needed, but the station tries to fundraise the amount, £50,000, that it costs. They were given two years to raise the money, and after eight months were already asking what else they should be raising money for, because they had hit their target: 'And that's because wives, mums, grandparents, people who don't have any blood relation involved but just want to be a part of the fundraising team got involved and donated money.' All of this is a testament to what the RNLI represents. 'We get kids that sell sea glass outside the station, and we even get kids in the middle of Northamptonshire, who have drawn pictures or sold stuff outside Tesco, and who turn up with a £100 cheque or a £10 cheque. So from the remotest, most landlocked parts of the country through to the coasts where we live, there's this deep-rooted romance and love for an organisation that does what we do.'

Damien calls the RNLI 'one of the chambers of the heart of the village', but as I talk to him about all this I think it's more than that: it's the actual soul of the place. You can see it in the old pictures: on the wall of the lifeboat station is a fantastic black and white photo from the 1930s, back in the days when the wives of the crew used to give piggybacks to their husbands to get them out to the boat so they wouldn't get their feet wet before they went to sea. The picture shows the *Richard and Sarah*, the lifeboat back then, being towed through the village by two lines of men on ropes, their backs hunched with the effort. The streets are so narrow that the sides of the boat are grazing the walls of the houses, and it looks as though every man in the village has turned out to play his part, such was the importance of the lifeboat and its crew. It's the community spirit there to see in black and white. The walls of the lifeboat station are hung with picture after picture of crews past and present; often men and women from the same families, generation after generation turning out to do the same vital job. Ordinary men and women who were willing to put their lives on the line when it was needed. And who in doing so not only saved lives but gave a lifeblood to the community they represented.

I've written about Damien and the Port Isaac RNLI here because I know them and admire them and they are close to my heart. But in truth, the humble heroes of this piece are not just the guys from the Port Isaac crew. Damien and his team are just one representation of a network of heroes that runs up and down the whole country. There are 238 lifeboat stations around the UK and Ireland, including the busiest one of all – Tower station in the heart of London – and Aith, the most northerly station, right up in Shetland. Each one of these 238 stations has a crew as dedicated as Port Isaac's. Each one has its Damiens and its Matts and its Nickys, ready and willing to jump in a boat and risk themselves to help others. And each in its own way represents the community it protects.

'The RNLI will never die,' says Damien, and with heroes like him and his crew at its heart, I am sure he is right.

The Orchard Project

'There's something about orchards that sort of resonates with humans, speaks to our hearts,' says Kath Rosen, the current CEO of The Orchard Project. 'We can all visualise what an orchard is, a beautiful place where there's abundance, and there's a way to connect with nature in a spiritual way.' Orchards, as she says, bring us back somehow to the garden of Eden: whoever we are, across all cultures, there's somehow a folk memory that makes an orchard an inviting, enriching place. I agree with her, but most of us would probably associate those images with green fields and countryside, not with pavements, high rises and inner cities. But The Orchard Project is doing something rather wonderful. Its ultimate aim is a simple but far-reaching one – plant enough fruit trees that everyone in urban areas is within walking distance of a thriving orchard. It is bringing a bit of the rural idyll into inner-city areas, and perhaps more importantly, creating new communities along the way.

This lovely idea started in 2009, born out of a moment when one of the founders was jogging in a London park and, looking around at the trees, wondered what the scene might be like if the Victorians had planted fruit trees rather than ornamental ones. What effect might that have on Londoners – to be able to go and pick an apple wherever they lived? From that original seed, The Orchard Project was born, starting first of all on a small site in Hackney. From there the project has grown, until it has now supported over 540 communities in planting their orchards, from Edinburgh and Glasgow to Manchester, Liverpool, Cardiff, London and beyond. That's a lot of apple trees planted – and not just apples but pears, plums, medlars... It's a mouth-watering list.

Over the last years, the awareness of the need for biodiversity has grown, and 'rewilding' has become part of the national consciousness. The word usually makes you think of acres and acres of grand estate land returned to nature, but The Orchard Project is doing rewilding on a different and no less rewarding scale. Take Kath's description of an unloved area in Hackney, originally a rubbish-ridden patch of grass round an estate, that was transformed first of all by the planting of the orchard: 'Then they got really into the idea of rewilding the area around it, so they've put ponds, hedges, underplanting. It's become this kind of nature oasis, and been commended as a site of nature conservation in Hackney.' What a wonderful image – the complete transformation of a patch of waste ground into something humming with life.

★

How does it work? The new orchards – not huge, often just five to ten trees at a time – take under-loved scraps of urban space and turn them into something thriving and healthy. The headline benefits are clear – improved urban landscape, a chance for biodiversity to flourish, more shade, more water retention... They are just a force for good. But it is perhaps the community benefits that are most exciting. A founding principle of The Orchard Project is that they always wait to be invited in, not just by one or two individuals, but by the wider local community. 'We never go to people and say, "You need an orchard here",' says Kath.

It's important that the impetus comes from the community, because a huge amount of the work involved is in the aftercare, not in the planting of an orchard: 'There has to be ownership and willingness. We want to know they've consulted, and that there's appetite to have those trees there.'

That aftercare is particularly important: Kath lets me in on a depressing statistic – according to the Forestry Commission, 40–50 per cent of newly planted urban trees die. 'There's this massive tree-planting agenda and half those trees are being wasted. It's down to aftercare and the really difficult conditions those trees are in.' This is why whenever The Orchard Project is invited in to plant an orchard with a community, they undertake to support those trees for at least five years. This transforms the tree survival rate out of all recognition – to 95 per cent – and also enables perhaps the most important thing that The Orchard Project does, which is to promote community cohesion and education. Because it might look like what the project does is about the trees, but in fact it's pretty clear that, in the end, it's all about people.

'What we exist to do is to give people the skills to look after the fruit trees and all the things that go with that, rather than putting the trees in the ground,' says Kath. The charity runs education courses where people can get serious accreditations at a GCSE equivalent level in forest gardening and community orcharding: people have been through those courses and come back to work or volunteer for the charity, or found employment elsewhere in the green sector. Perhaps even more valuably, they run workshops, volunteer days and training sessions: wonderful opportunities for communities to come together. There are family days and celebratory events, gatherings and parties, wassails and fruit blessing ceremonies. Anything that brings the neighbourhood together and promotes the orchards.

★

They have also restored a huge number of veteran orchards, and undertaken a three-year project in London to restore 30 neglected dwindling orchards to their former glory. These orchards, often attached to the sites of old monasteries or the grounds of hospitals, tend to have wonderful historic significance: their restoration gained the Best Heritage Project award from the National Lottery in 2019. It was a real labour of love. And one with a particularly welcome side product: it is in these orchards that there tends to be a glut of fruit, a problem neatly solved by a partnership with a cider company to produce 'Local Fox' cider. Every can bought supports the cause! They have also entered into a partnership with the Ministry of Justice to plant an orchard in every prison.

As a charity, The Orchard Project prides itself on being versatile and adaptable, tailoring its approach to whatever the community needs. It's also constantly on the move, thinking up new ideas and initiatives. At the moment, it is in the planning stages of larger-scale orchards, which will be more than oases – they will be 'food forests'. In three different pilot sites, they are planting different edible species alongside the trees – there will be 'plants at all levels of the canopy, so at the bottom you might have strawberries or plants that will help pollinate the trees… raspberries or vines around the trees… lots of nut trees, and edible hedges surrounding it all.' It sounds like a mediaeval vision of plenty. And when you consider the 'fresh food desserts' that beset some of our inner cities, it is a project that has the capacity to transform how people who are cut off from access to good ingredients think about their food. The brilliant benefits to the orchards seem to go on and on.

In the end, though, it is the people who matter – the community who gather to plant and feed and mulch and water the infant trees, who learn how to care for them and to tend them. Kath has seen the bonds it has created between all sorts of people, old and young, from every different culture. It's such a lovely image, the building of a new kind of connection at the feet of these tiny nascent trees: 'Orchards often act as a catalyst for other things, so the trees are the infrastructure and then other community projects spring up around them. It might be community growing or a community kitchen, all sorts of things. We do quite a lot of impact assessment on individual wellbeing, and being involved in these projects is hugely beneficial.' I can well believe it. What better way to be rooted in the community and the earth than watching the green shoots turn to blossom, year in, year out? Feeling the benefits of growing, learning the skills, tending a patch of ground that will become a hub for the neighbourhood. And all this in the heart of cities. It's amazing what some time, care and apple trees can do.

'We'd like to see them everywhere,' says Kath. 'If you're going to plant a tree, make it an edible one.'

Shelley Hart

I'm an Essex boy at heart. I grew up in Epping, and I spent a lot of my life round Woodford and the surrounding area. So I know full well first-hand what a fantastic county it is, and how warm the sense of community is there. Not to mention how there is a certain type of Essex woman who through sheer warmth, determination and energy can absolutely move mountains. But even I was bowled over to meet Shelley Hart, who encapsulates all of these qualities, and more. Not that she'd be keen to award any of those accolades to herself. For Shelley, it's all about the team she leads as the founder and CEO of Havering Volunteer Centre, an organisation that in just seven short years has brightened the lives of so many people, and given help and support to hundreds of organisations.

The story of the Havering Volunteer Centre began in 2015. At the time, Shelley was a volunteer centre manager at another organisation, and when she found it was closing, she was aghast. Listening to the dismay of the volunteers and organisations who were mutually benefitting from the organisation, she asked a simple question: 'If I were to set up on my own, do you think that's viable and would you come with me?' The answer was a resounding yes. For Shelley, that was all she needed to hear: using Costa Coffee as her office, and a blank sheet of paper as her starting point, she got to work. From that acorn, a seriously impressive organisation began to grow, one that currently links around 4,000 volunteers with about 400 voluntary organisations. Those numbers sound pretty impressive, but not as impressive as this one: in seven years, the HVC has saved the economy of Havering around £22 million in volunteer hours. Just think about it – £22 million! That is a simply astonishing figure.

Shelley has been involved with volunteering since she was a girl, and she is evangelical about its benefits, for the individuals and organisations who are helped, and especially for the volunteers themselves. Over and over again she has seen the effects of volunteering. People come to be volunteers for all sorts of reasons, and she has seen what it has done for people who have come through the worst of circumstances – who have had crises of mental or physical health, who have come out of abusive relationships, or who are struggling with self-esteem or are in recovery. She knows that getting the right volunteer in the right place can transform lives: 'We've put them on the next level of their journey; we've seen them flourish and grow and gain employment, or set up businesses for themselves, and just have connections with people again.'

★

If Havering Volunteer Centre is a fantastic resource in normal times, it won't surprise you to hear that during the pandemic the services it offered became even more invaluable. Even to someone as experienced as Shelley – she mentions almost in passing that as a member of Victim Support she helped with the fallout of the 7/7 bombings, and later as a volunteer on the effects of Grenfell – the scale of what was needed came as a shock.

In the months leading up to the first lockdown of 2020 she had been tracking the pandemic, because everything she had learned during those previous disasters warned her that the volunteer sector was going to play a crucial part in whatever was coming. She got as ready as she could be – by 17th March 2020, a week before the first lockdown, she already had a volunteer army ready to go – but the sheer volume of calls that started to come in threatened to overwhelm even the resources she had put together. In a normal year the centre takes about 5,000 calls from people wanting to get involved. That year the number went up to 29,000 and the nature of the conversations changed. 'We were taking 400 calls a day, crisis calls. We didn't know what was going to be at the end of that call when they phoned us. Some people hadn't spoken to a soul for weeks and it just opened my eyes to the level of loneliness in our community,' she says. Even Shelley was surprised to see how deep this ran – not just among older people, but in every age group and demographic.

The stories that the team started to hear were heartbreaking – there were people whose only social interactions in normal times were with the checkout lady at Tesco, or the person behind the counter at the local coffee shop. When even that was ripped away from them the isolation threatened to be unbearable. Shelley's solution was to set up a 'Check in and Chat' buddy system. Within ten days, 600 people signed up to help: some of them were people who were shielding and isolated themselves, but wanted to do what they could to help others. She's proud to say that some of those connections continue to this day, some with just a weekly check-in phone call, some who have formed strong and lasting friendships.

But that was only the tip of the iceberg: the centre linked up those who were suddenly furloughed or made redundant because of Covid with those who were in need. Understanding how bereft and lacking in hope people who were suddenly out of work were, she got them involved as volunteers in everything from picking up food and medicines to walking dogs because the owners couldn't get out and about, or going to hospitals to collect people's hearing aids because they hadn't been able to hear for weeks – it's not something you might think about, but losing that ability to hear was of course a total disaster during the isolation of the pandemic.

Not to mention, of course, the invaluable help the centre gave to the vaccination effort. When I ask her whether she placed volunteers in vaccine centres, Shelley's answer is immediate: '724, to be precise, over two centres!' One of those centres was considered the best in the country. Not only did she and her team place 100 volunteers on site each day, matching each of the different roles – car park marshals, greeters, checkers – with the right person, they also managed the rotas themselves. It was a huge job, one that was meant to last for six weeks, and went on for 15 months: 'There was such a lot of devastation around, but by volunteering, people could feel good about themselves because they were brightening someone else's day.' And in the midst of the terrible hardship caused to communities by the lockdowns, she was also in a prime position to see that small seeds of hope were being sown, a sense of connection with the community was growing. She noticed people connecting back with their communities in a new way, really looking at their neighbours and taking care of their needs. It's important to her that we don't slip back, that we learn the lesson that things are a lot easier when we face them together.

Like so many of the humble heroes I have met while putting together this book, Shelley is a firm believer in the magical mathematics of helping other people: 'If we can help one person that may then be able to pay that forward, then we've helped two people, and it goes on that way.' She saw this in action recently with one of their volunteers who came to them during the pandemic, after he was furloughed and then made redundant. He has now gone on to set up his own business, one that employs two people, one as a trainee who he is helping through his apprenticeship. So that's three lives improved by one person volunteering: 'It ripples right through the community, the power of good.'

The key to the power of Havering Volunteer Centre as an organisation, Shelley believes, is that it doesn't just match a volunteer with a role and leave it there. She and her team are always listening, always making sure that they follow up with volunteers and ensure things are going well. 'They don't actually leave us until they say, "Don't bother us any more"!' she says with a laugh. And the holistic approach they take means that they can find the perfect role for everyone who walks through their doors. One man who came to them saying he just wanted to deliver leaflets was given a role doing exactly that. But gradually, as they got to know him, they realised his passion and skill for music, at a time when it just so happened that the local hospital was looking for someone to play piano in their atrium. From then on, until the pandemic put it on pause, every Friday afternoon he would go and take up his position at the piano in the foyer, welcoming every person who came through the hospital doors. When Shelley was visiting one day for an event, he spotted and asked her what music she'd like him to play for her.

'I like Billy Joel,' she said. When he looked a bit uncertain she reassured him: 'Don't worry, just play me anything' – and enjoyed the Beatles medley he played as she got on with her work. That was, until halfway through when she heard him break into a Billy Joel song, and suddenly found herself in floods of tears.

'I've got a tingle now, just thinking about it. The magic that was coming out of this man's fingers, and he doesn't realise the joy he is bringing to people just by playing that music. And that is the beauty of people. They just don't know what's inside them.'

Another volunteer who had had some mobility issues because of illness came to drop off some supplies when the centre was collecting for the Afghan crisis. Seeing how much was needed to be done, he ended up staying to help (they had received over a thousand bags of donations in just two days). He ended up staying five months to sort everything out, and becoming an invaluable part of the team. Even better, they discovered he was a whizz at IT, inspiring the centre to set up an IT buddy scheme where he could help people with their tablets and phones. Not only a valuable service but one that gave him a renewed sense of purpose: 'That's what volunteering does, it makes you you again. It makes you whole and it just lifts people's spirits.'

It's just invigorating, talking to Shelley: there's so much passion and joy and fun embedded in the way she approaches everything she does. Considering she started all this in a coffee shop with a blank piece of paper, it's quite something to see her sitting at the nerve centre of this fantastic organisation and hearing all about what the organisation has achieved. But it's pretty hard to get her to blow her own trumpet: as far as she's concerned it's all about the fantastic people around her, people who, like her, were doing ten-hour days, weekdays and weekends over the pandemic: 'I've got a massive support network. I've got great family, wonderful volunteers, a wonderful team here. And we feed off each other and we just love helping people.'

It's also pretty clear that she doesn't have much time to sit back and reflect on her achievements: she's got too much still to do. But there are definitely moments. Sometimes she will meet someone who will fling their arms around her and tell her that the centre changed their lives, or she will hear that someone who had been out of work for ages aced an interview because of the joy with which they talked about their volunteering experience. And there are times when the enormity of the undertaking particularly through the pandemic, really hits her: 'You do sometimes think, Imagine. Imagine what it would be like if we hadn't been here and helped those thousands of people and those thousands of families. They would still be lonely. They would still be lost.'

At the Havering Volunteer Centre they have a motto: 'Be that difference, be that change, be that person who does it'. It's why the symbol of the centre is a jaunty little bee. And I can't help but think of Shelley as that incredibly busy bee herself, constantly working and helping, and brightening so many lives as she does so. Thank goodness for her, and for others like her: all the people who bring joy to the business of making the world a better place.

Ryan Bannerman

When David Forbes saw that I had put out a call on social media for people to nominate their own humble heroes, he didn't hesitate for a second. He knew exactly who he thought deserved the recognition. David is a bit of a hero himself, given his role as leader at Future Choices, which is a charity he founded in his home city of Aberdeen, to provide social interaction and inclusion and recreation for disabled people. Future Choices is entirely staffed by volunteers, and it is very much a team enterprise, so David is surrounded by people who are good at going above and beyond for their community. But the person who first sprang to mind as his humble hero was Ryan Bannerman.

Ryan is still only 16 years old, but he has been volunteering in his community since he was 12. I asked David what it was that made him think of Ryan, and his answer was simple: 'Ryan from an early age has just wanted to help his community. Regardless of what sector, whether homeless or disabled, he just wants to make a difference.' That's something that's worth celebrating on its own, but David also has a little bit of an ulterior motive. He's seen the bad press that young people sometimes get, and he knows there is a whole other side to the coin: 'We hear so many bad stories, let's hear a really nice story of a young lad just wanting to make a difference.'

Talking to Ryan himself, I totally agree. If Shelley Hart down in Essex is one of the people who are driving the amazing engine that is the volunteer sector, then it is people like Ryan, up and down the country, who provide the fuel. Ryan first started out helping at Future Choices when he was just 12, and ever since then, he says, he 'just wanted to make a difference in the world.' At just 13, he had an idea which was a stroke of genius: he thought about the instant win tokens that people could win through the McDonald's Monopoly promotion. People buy their meal and get a token which might win an extra portion of fries or a drink. But, reckoned Ryan, who needed that extra portion more – the person who was already getting their McDonald's, or someone on the street who was hungry and homeless? He managed to persuade people to part with their tokens, and he and his mate collected 150 tokens that year to give to a charity that helps with the homeless. I think it's just a brilliantly simple idea, but Ryan is characteristically modest about it. 'I just think it's a good thing to do,' he says.

Most of Ryan's volunteering work centres around Future Choices itself, which is a wonderful charity, one of those organisations that makes a huge difference to the lives of people who are too easily forgotten in society. As a carer for his disabled mother, David was driven to setting it up back in 2008 when their previous social hub, Choices, closed down. Since then, it has gone on to provide an absolutely vital resource –

giving to people who may otherwise be stuck in their houses permanently the promise that once a week they will get that sense of warmth, connection and fun that makes us human. It is a service that has grown from just a handful of visitors when it started to a reliably full hall every single week, and it simply could not happen without the close team of volunteers that David has gathered. David is keen to bring young people on board, well aware that the future of all volunteer organisations lies with the next generation.

Ever since he started at the age of 12, Ryan has been a vital part of that, gaining more and more hours of volunteering to gain his Saltire Awards, which reward young people doing volunteer work in Scotland. David knows too that the best way to get the youth involved is for people like Ryan to show the way: if you want to cut through and persuade young folks into volunteering, the message is going to come across much better from Ryan and his friends than from any adult.

I love the idea of the Saltire Awards: someone like Ryan is absolutely the proof that getting young people into volunteering works, because he is absolutely passionate about it. The way he sees things, there are people out there who just need a bit of extra help, and how great to be the person who is giving it. 'Having a conversation with them will make their day,' he says, 'It's 20 minutes out of your life, but maybe way more for them in their mind because they are stuck in their house.' From his side of the coin, he believes he's had so much life experience, something that he can put on his CV later on. And above all, 'It makes me feel like a good person that can help others.' When I ask him what he wants to do in life, he says he wants to stay involved with Future Choices – 'He's after my job!' jokes David – but Ryan is hoping to become a mechanic. He knows that whatever he does he will use the skills he has learned, whether that's talking to people from all walks of life, or knowing how to give someone mobility help.

Though he is only 16, David is about to give Ryan a significant step up for someone that is so young, as assistant manager for the fundraising popup shop that Future Choices will run in summer 2022. He's going to have to learn a lot for the role, 'Leadership, delegation, all the things that happen when you're a manager,' says David. He's a firm believer in pushing people out of their comfort zones to get the best out of them, and he knows that Ryan will handle any challenge thrown at him.

'You work with so many young people and then there's just that one person that shines, and that for me is Ryan: he just shines. They're all amazing, all the young people doing community work are great, but Ryan just has that *je ne sais quoi*.'

As for Ryan, not only has he caught the volunteering bug himself, but he's always keen to spread the word: 'I'd say give it a go. If you give it a go and you don't like it, you don't like it, but volunteering gives you a lot. I'd say you are going to like it.'

I don't doubt for a second that Ryan will continue doing what he's doing, giving his time to others. As he says, 'Five hundred hours of volunteering – it doesn't feel like that. It feels like I've been doing it for one day, it's so addictive.'

I just love to see someone of Ryan's age getting stuck in the way he does. And it just blows me away that he's learned so young what some of us don't realise until we are much longer in the tooth – that you get as much from helping people as they get from you. That's a piece of knowledge that is just priceless.

Aaron Hill

Every Saturday and Sunday, up and down the country, football pitches and sports clubs are full of kids having a great time, getting exercise, letting off steam, learning skills and forging friendships. I was definitely one of those kids – rugby was my sport – but I'm not sure that at the time I fully appreciated quite how much effort and behind-the-scenes work the volunteer coaches had to put in to keep this whole enormous machine ticking over. Now that I'm an adult and understand what it takes to have a full-time job and all the other responsibilities in life, I am in awe of those many, many people who willingly give their free time and so much effort to make sure that these grassroots teams are thriving and that kids can have these great experiences. I genuinely believe that the difference volunteer coaches can make to a community and a child's life is just enormous.

Back when I was playing rugby as a kid, the absolute lynchpin of Woodford Rugby Club was Harold Collie, who ran the minis section for the under-sevens. He was the headmaster at one of the local schools, and just incredibly passionate about rugby. Every week, after a full week's work, he would be there on Sunday, come rain or come shine. He set the template for the entire rugby club in the end – the minis section were such a success that as they grew, they fed into the older teams. His name still resonates for anyone who was involved with WRC. As do the names of the other coaches – not least my dad David Shephard (obviously), but also Roger Langdell, Ivan Loftman… These were people that were so important to me growing up, and I still have incredibly fond memories of them all.

Which is why I am absolutely delighted to meet Aaron Hill, who is a stalwart of the Tonbridge Junior Football Club and has been for over 15 years. I think all the volunteer coaches who take on this kind of role are amazing, but there is an additional way in which Aaron has made a real difference.

It all started around five years ago, when his son, who had been involved with the club for years, was coming to the end of his youth training. It dawned on Aaron that although officially the club ran mixed teams, there was at that point just one girl left in the whole club. That is one girl, out of 450 players. Not a great statistic. Aaron decided that needed to change, and so he took it upon himself to set up a girls' team. The reaction from inside the club was a bit sceptical: there had been initiatives before to bring girls in, but they had all dwindled. The general consensus was that there wouldn't be enough girls who would be interested. Aaron felt a bit bullish about it. 'There was an element probably of stubbornness,' he says.

Of course, in this day and age it seems ridiculous that this should even be an issue. Nevertheless, these attitudes do still remain: there are people who automatically assume that girls should be doing ballet and boys playing football. Or if the girls do want to play, they are given that much less respect – they'll probably give it up, goes the reasoning, or they can just join the boys' team. This made no sense to Aaron, who just saw a huge part of the community not being served and a huge amount of potential being wasted.

The first step was an open day. Four girls turned up. 'Well', thought Aaron, 'that's four girls who want to do something.' So he started from there. The first girls who came tended to be the sisters of boys who were already playing in the club and wanted to have a go: Aaron's own daughter Emily was one of these. She did ballet, but she also really wanted to be part of the club that her brother loved so much. As these first girls started to enjoy it, they brought in their friends, and as they did their training sessions in the local park, more and more people started to see the girls having a great time and wanted to join in: 'Once you start it's like a snowball, you roll it and roll it and then it grows. It was just a case of believing we can get there and don't worry about some little bumps in the road.'

That open day, with four girls turning up, happened just five years ago. Now, there are 140 girls playing for Tonbridge Junior Football Club, across ten teams. They are the second-biggest girls' football club in the whole of Kent, play in the local Kent league, and have become so popular that they struggle to find enough pitches to play on.

Aaron may modestly say that this snowball effect just happened once things got started, but I'm pretty sure that it wouldn't have done if it hadn't been for his own passion and determination. Think how much time and effort and enthusiasm went into building up those teams – planning the training, putting it on, arranging the fixtures, organising the girls... it's an endless job, and to top it off, Aaron is now also on the committee of the Kent Girls League. It was Aaron's wife, Nicola, who nominated him when I asked people to think about their humble heroes, because she has seen for herself the work that goes into it all – every evening spent on a laptop with football-related issues, every Saturday and Sunday taken up with training. You can only put that amount in if you're really passionate about something, but look how much the girls get out of it. It's not just a sport, it's more than that – it's confidence, pride and friendship. This was something that Nicola, who is a teacher, particularly noticed during the pandemic – those girls who were transferring from primary to secondary through that really difficult time, including her own daughter, found that the support and friendships they had made through the club made a real difference.

Great clubs don't just happen haphazardly – they take a lot of thought and planning. Starting where he did, Aaron put a lot of care into how the teams should be formed. He was determined that the girls' teams should have really strong foundations, which meant that at first he particularly encouraged the younger players – the under-nines and under-11s. He knew that jumping in and trying to start an under-14s team from scratch was likely to lead to disappointment – they would end up playing teams who had five years' edge on them in terms of experience. 'It's not much fun if you're getting battered 10–nil,' he says. He wanted the teams to have time to develop their skills and enjoy the game, so for the first year they played only friendlies. It was all about building the team from the bottom up. Aaron still remembers the first time they got the teams out for a proper match: it happened to be an absolutely pouring wet day, so when the girls came off, 'they were covered in mud and drenched to their bones, but the smiles on their faces: you just couldn't beat it.' It was at that moment that Aaron thought, 'We've got something here.'

He is also adamant that the spirit the game is played in should be a really positive one. Everyone involved with the teams shares the attitude, so you don't get those 'shouty, quite embarrassing coaches' yelling from the sidelines. The teams have won various tournaments and shields, but he is also particularly proud that they have won sportsmanship awards for their attitudes over entire seasons. Aaron believes that this positivity is a big draw and the reason that the team has become so popular, and I am sure it springs from Aaron himself. He talks about the team with such joy that it's no wonder the girls look up to him. Clearly that contagious enthusiasm has rubbed off at home: his son is now at university, studying football coaching as a degree. 'The whole family's got involved,' says Nicola.

It sounds like Aaron is so busy (his day job is as a town planner) that there almost isn't time to stand back and think about what he has achieved. But sometimes, going down to the sports ground on a Sunday, it will really hit him. Depending on the way the fixtures fall on any one weekend, sometimes on a Sunday there will more girls' matches than boys' – there may be up to seven teams all playing at once. Looking around at those teams of girls so determined and engaged in their sport, my guess is that Aaron can't help but be proud of what he started. Indeed, sometimes the thought runs through his mind: 'Wow, that's some going, that is.'

None of that scene would be there if he hadn't made that decision five years ago to change things up and get girls just as involved in the club as the boys were. He's not a man to wear his achievements on his sleeve – when he heard he was one of my humble heroes, says Nicola, the very first thing he said was, 'Why me? I'm not special, I'm not important.'

But I believe he really is important. For me, he represents all those coaches and volunteers and parents up and down the country, manning the sidelines at football clubs and cricket clubs and rugby clubs and all the other sporting endeavours. It is because of people like Aaron that ambitions are nurtured, communities grow, potential is realised. Those 140 girls flying round the football pitches every weekend are having fun, first and foremost. And my guess is they don't put a lot of thought into how much work has gone on behind the scenes to make that happen (which is just as it should be). Who knows where those girls will end up? Perhaps on those football pitches there's a future England captain? Or perhaps they will just go on to be fabulous people who know how to be brilliant team players. Either way, I bet that, just like I did, they will come away with some wonderful memories – and will always be grateful to the man who made it happen.

heroes of
innovation

Team UnLimbited

You may have seen some of the videos online. If not, I urge you to go and look them up: each one is just a shot of pure joy. The places and people differ, but the central themes remain the same: the template is laid down in the first one, titled simply 'Isabella'. Sitting in her sitting room at home, Isabella sits next to her mother, excitedly opening a large box wrapped in shiny pink paper. Her name is written on a label inside, in large green letters underneath a heart. Delving into the packing beans, Isabella pulls out a curious-looking contraption, styled in a way that is guaranteed to strike happiness into the heart of any young girl: purple and pink and green plastic. It's clear from her expression that this is one of the best presents she's ever received.

The contraption is an artificial arm, but it's not like any arm you've seen before. Like a cross between something from the best comic ever and a sci-fi movie, this is something colourful and fun and absolutely appropriate for a seven-year-old girl. Without any hesitation, Isabella takes the arm in her right hand. Within moments it is strapped in place with Velcro straps, and Isabella, beaming, is watching delightedly as she opens and closes the pink and purple fingers on her new left hand. I defy you not to have tears in your eyes when she turns behind her and picks up a toy figurine on the windowsill, a smile as wide as the sun on her face.

In other videos, you watch as children intently scramble to open their presents – always wrapped in cheerful paper – and pull out from inside them rainbow arms, superhero arms, arms in the colours of their favourite football strips, arms in every colour and design combination you can think of. Over the course of the videos the devices get sleeker, neater, more streamlined, but in each one you see the same thing: the joy and curiosity with which the children greet their new limbs ('so light!'), the speed with which they strap them on, the cheers and applause from the parents, the growing amazement in the children's eyes, and the wonderful moment when they go to pick up a toy or play with their LEGO. Then there are the pictures of the kids, arms now fully in place, just being kids: throwing a ball for their dog, or cycling with confidence, both hands on the handlebars of their bikes. In one picture, a young girl plays a cello, bow held in a colourful grip. They look like the essence of childhood. I could watch them all day.

The men behind these moments of joy are Steve Davies and Drew Murray, otherwise known as Team UnLimbited. It is in Steve's Willy Wonka-like garden shed that these devices are made, built by 3D printers in multicoloured plastic, from designs developed by both of them and their technical and 3D printing skills. Together, these two men have cast their magic even further than you might imagine.

I first came across them in 2017, when Steve's extremely modest shed was featured on *Shed of the Year* on Channel 4. Like everyone else, I was blown away by what was hidden inside that bog-standard (and rather tiny) construction: a mad factory conjuring up multicoloured contraptions that change children's lives for the better. Which is why I'm particularly delighted that when I talk to Steve and Drew over Zoom one afternoon, Steve is coming to me live from inside his shed – now updated and improved after a company was inspired by the programme to donate a new one. Hanging on the walls behind him are various parts and gadgets. The whole place is lit by a bluish glow from the 3D printer to give that extra air of otherworldliness, and it is fantastic to know that all this magic is brewed up between this shed and Drew's home, hundreds of miles away.

One quite extraordinary thing about Steve and Drew's partnership is that though they have worked together seamlessly for seven years, most of their collaboration has been remote: they have rarely been in the same room. Nonetheless, they are fully in tune with each other, picking up each other's train of thought, clearly totally in sync with their dreams for Team UnLimbited. Their partnership has grown organically, born out of their shared skills and approach, and it is clear how much they both care about the same things, both the intricacies of design and the real purpose of what they are doing.

Underlying it all perhaps is the profound understanding that Steve has of the challenges and problems their customers face. He was born with no left hand, and so is absolutely familiar with the kind of prosthetics that are available from the NHS. There's the dummy hand, that looks realistic in a plasticky way, but doesn't do anything; or the hook hand that is functional in a basic way but looks terrible. As a child he was even a tester for the myoelectric hand that the NHS were trialling at the time as their version of the robotic hand. 'They all had one thing in common,' Steve says now, 'None of them made me feel any good about myself. Everybody I've ever met who has worn them says the same thing – they're too heavy, they're too hot when you put them on, when you've got them on sometimes they're too difficult to get off if you're sweaty. And nobody I know has ever felt like it's lifted their spirits.'

As an adult, Steve had in fact stopped using any prosthetics at all, but when he became a father he thought that he perhaps needed something to help with dad-style tasks like lawn mowing and using hedge trimmers. So he went back to the NHS, with some reluctance because he is an independent spirit who doesn't like to ask for help. But the hand they gave him actually reduced him to tears. It harked back to the hands of his childhood; it was 'like something from a mediaeval torture chamber'. He shows it to me: steel rods, an off-putting claw, a clunky, pinkish plastic arm grip. I definitely see his point.

When Steve despairingly posted a picture of the NHS arm online, Drew picked up on it through an online partnership programme he was involved in that matched his 3D printing skills with people in need of it. It was a bit of a departure for Drew: 'I thought, "I've always made devices for children, I'll make one for this 40-year-old guy in Swansea."' As they began to collaborate, Steve, who is a trained CAD (computer-aided design) operator, started sending files for Drew to print, tweaking this element or improving that, and Drew realised that Steve had a unique perspective: he understood the needs of the user and he also had the technical knowledge of how the machinery should operate. When Steve finally received his hand, it was like nothing he had ever tried before. Rather than hiding his hand away in a pocket as he had always done, he wanted to show it off to the world. It was an extraordinary liberation from the emotional burden and self-consciousness he had always felt.

'The day I received the hand that Drew built me was one of the greatest days of my life,' he says. It gave him such a feeling of confidence that he immediately knew he wanted to share that experience with others, to help pass on the gift that he had been given. And that was what led him to Isabella: he agreed to do for her what Drew had done for him, and to make an arm for her in her favourite colours – pink and purple and green. So with Drew coaching him in the intricacies of 3D printing, Steve set about it. ('It nearly killed him, building that arm,' says Drew, laughing.)

Both Steve and Drew are alike in that they are natural problem-solvers, always looking for every single small way to make the devices better. Take that very first arm, the one Steve made for Isabella: Steve made it in the colours she had requested, watching her open it was amazing. It's emotional enough to watch it as one of the many thousands who have seen it online – imagine how it felt for Steve, who knew just what that gift meant for Isabella, and who was in the room when she tried it on. It was a fantastic moment. 'But ultimately, I came away from that meeting thinking, "This isn't good enough. It isn't as good as it could be."' That was where Team

UnLimbited was really born, because together, he and Drew decided to work on the design to change that, and make every element as perfect as possible. They spent months and months improving, tweaking, trying to make the design as simple as they could. When they were as satisfied as they could be, they made another arm in Isabella's signature colours and took it back to her – another wonderful moment you can see online – and from that moment version one of the Team UnLimbited arm – the Isabella Edition – was born.

What makes the Team UnLimbited arm so effective? For a start, its simplicity. It's not an electronic device – the fingers are operated by a pulley system operated by the movements of the wrist or elbow. You bend the joint, the hand closes, bend it back and the hand opens. 'There's no electronics, no expensive motors. We only require some string and some elastic and some Velcro,' says Steve. All the static components of the arm are plastic, and can be printed on any 3D printer. And the thing that lifts the whole enterprise from hugely impressive to truly magical, for me, is that Steve and Drew have made the whole design of the arm open source. This means that anybody with access to a 3D printer, anywhere in the world, can go to their website, download the files, tweak a few simple measurements and create their own arm. All for the cost of the materials, which come to as little as £30.

Think about it: all those many thousands of hours that Steve and Drew have spent refining and perfecting their design are available to anybody anywhere who has the need. That just blows me away. But for Steve and Drew, it is absolutely fundamental to what they do. Says Steve: 'We made a decision very early on that we would never make a penny off this. As soon as you start going down that road, a hand that only cost £20 to build, all of a sudden costs £1,000 to sell.'

Drew agrees: 'There have been other people round the world who have been building devices and they have tried to do a bit of commercialisation on it and it always ends in tears because as soon as money comes into the equation, arguments are not far behind.' This attitude has meant that people around the world, from Chile to Indonesia, have benefitted from their work: 'There's nothing more special, sat here in my little workshop in my garden in Wales, than seeing a child in the middle of Africa or from Guatemala or Mexico or Syria or even the Himalayas using one of our arms. And they've done it through the kindness of someone who downloaded our free design and built it for them.'

In common with so many other of our humble heroes, one of the things that brings Steve and Drew the most joy is the way the effort they put in is so often paid forward – parents who have been gifted a printer to help their children will go on to make arms for others. It's a chain reaction, in some ways built into the DNA of their project, ever since Steve took the knowledge passed on from Drew and looked to see who he could help.

★

Affordability is a key component of the device for both of Steve and Drew. Not just because it makes it more accessible – there's a pretty huge difference between the £30-odd quid that their device costs and the £30,000 that you would need for a robotic arm – but because it allows families a flexibility that would otherwise be impossible. Studies have shown that lack of access to good artificial limbs in childhood leads to hugely increased rejection rates later in life for prosthetics. Parents doing their best to help their children with the challenges that limb difference brings are anxious to try everything they can. But £30,000 is not an outlay that most people can afford, not least because children outgrow their arms in the same way that they outgrow their clothes and shoes. And because they might simply not like them. 'Some children don't know whether they actually want an arm and it's a bit of a leap to say let's buy them a £30,000 robotic arm only to have them reject it,' says Steve. Instead, a Team UnLimbited device can either act as a first step to more sophisticated prosthetics, or they can decide it's not what they want and it can be put in the recycling. Either way is fine, because the way Team UnLimbited measure success is not counted in how the children use the arms, but in how they make them feel.

Some children, they find, will wear this new part of themselves every single day and come back for more. Some will only wear it once or twice, and decide that they can do just as well without. For Drew, this in itself is success, because although the arms are functional, functionality is not the fundamental point. What is more important for the guys is the psychological boost the arms can bring. This is why involving the children in the design process is a key part of it all. That way, the arms feel like an extension of the children themselves, something they can show off and have fun with. 'The devices are designed by them, so they *are* them,' says Drew. 'It's not a doll-like prosthetic arm, it's me.' For Steve, this makes the design element one of the best parts of the process, getting to hear about the children and their families, getting a sense of who they are, making sure that the finished devices really represent them. The requests he gets are incredibly varied – from superhero (and supervillain) gauntlets to glow-in-the-dark arms. 'We even built an urban camouflage arm for a 90-year-old woman,' says Steve, 'and she loved it.' All of this joy is encapsulated in the way the children are given their arms: this isn't a clinical, medical procedure in a hospital setting; this is a child receiving a gift, wrapped in festive paper, a parcel filled with anticipation.

In a way, for Drew, the ultimate success would be for the children to realise that in the end limb difference doesn't really matter. What matters is that the child has had the experience, has had the opportunity to understand that 'they are actually a highly functional person, and that what you achieve is from your self-belief.' If some brightly coloured piece of plastic can help a child stop hiding away or losing their self-esteem or being held back by their sense of difference, then it doesn't matter whether it is used every day of their lives, or ends up as a piece of decoration on their bedroom shelf.

And the reports they get back from the parents reflect exactly what they are trying to achieve – there are stories about children who disliked going to the shops because they didn't like the stares, who are now out and proud and dying to show their new arms off. Kids who have been bullied and who now find their peers are jealous of their cool new piece of kit. Kids whose schools want to do an assembly about them, so they can demonstrate their devices to their friends. It's interesting that Drew and Steve hear from some parents that until the kids bring their new arms in to show off, their schools have never directly mentioned that the children have limb difference. They just haven't known how to address it until suddenly the new arm becomes a talking point and opens the conversation up.

★

Team UnLimbited has garnered praise from all sorts of quarters: the guys have visited Downing Street and Buckingham Palace, and their arm has even been displayed in the Science Museum in London (where Drew's proud father celebrated it by dragging every single passer-by over to the cabinet to show off what his son had made). After Steven's *Shed of the Year* appearance the public showed its stamp of approval not only by voting for him to win his category, but by donating to the cause – funds which they used to set up the charity, and which buoy it up to this day. But talking to the guys, you realise that the rewards for them aren't in any accolades or public recognition.

Take those videos I started out with: just like us, Steve and Drew can be moved to tears watching them. When a new arm reaches its recipient, says Steve, 'I spend the day pretty much crying because I know exactly what it is to go through it. I do it for the children because I've been there myself.' But beyond the tears, Steve and Drew are watching those videos with an eagle eye, seeing what tiny tweaks and improvements they can make, checking each and every feature to see it is doing the best job that it possibly can.

As we speak, they are already working away on version three, an arm that will be even simpler to build, and even smaller, allowing for younger recipients – Steve shows me the tiny hand, and it's amazing to think that a child as young as four may be able to use it one day. The challenges of the project are part of the joy of it all.

Ultimately, though, for them the real reward lies not just in the pleasure of the process, or even in the wonder and awe on the faces of the children – it is in the long-term impact their devices can have on the children's feelings about themselves, and how that in itself can help change their lives. That's quite an achievement to come out of the brains of two brilliant men, a 3D printer, and a garden shed.

Concrete4Change

There are some materials that are so ubiquitous that we almost stop noticing them. Go outside and look around, particularly if you are in a city, and you may not even register that a lot of what you are looking at is made of one particular thing: concrete. It is absolutely all around us. In fact, it is the most used material after water, and staggeringly, it currently accounts for 8 per cent of all global CO_2 emissions. And the thing is, because we are building more and more, just at the time we need to produce less and less carbon, this figure is predicted to rise to 40 per cent by 2050. Forty per cent! It makes you look at the average city street, building site or stretch of motorway with new eyes.

We all know that climate change is perhaps the most significant challenge that the world currently faces. It is one of those problems that can feel so overwhelming that it is difficult to see where the solutions lie – as every news programme reports on ever-worsening heatwaves across the world, forest fires, melting icecaps and more, the damage being done is so massive that it is hard to comprehend how to even start fixing it. That is why I love the idea of Concrete4Change, whose technology has the potential to make a difference on a global scale, by utilising and supercharging this most common of materials.

This potential breakthrough lies in a technological development, which would allow concrete to keep large amounts of CO_2 out of the atmosphere in perpetuity. Not only does it have the capacity to lock that carbon away, but in doing so it actually makes the concrete itself stronger, meaning that less has to be used, a win all round.

★

This game-changing technology is the brainchild of Dr Sid Pourfalah and Dr Michael Wise, an engineer specialising in concrete and a chemical engineer respectively, who came together to pool their extensive experience. Concrete does naturally sequester some CO_2 – what they realised was that there was a way of increasing this quality to lock up a significant proportion. The science is of course entirely beyond me, but 'essentially we are supercharging what concrete does naturally, developing a better version of concrete,' says Dr Aisling O'Loghlen, CFO of the company.

It sounds great, but the key question is how much CO_2 are we talking? When I put this question to Aisling, it takes me a moment to put her answer in context. The technology, she says, has the potential to permanently remove up to 2 billion tonnes of CO_2 by 2040, if the construction industry keeps growing at its current rate. What does that actually mean? 'It's the equivalent of total EU CO_2 emissions, an astronomical amount,' says Aisling. Let that sink in for a moment – if this concrete were to become the standard (and the technology can be used with any type of concrete), it would be able to lock up as much CO_2 as the whole of Europe currently produces. 'The first time we were delving into this ourselves among the team we had to double-check the figures,' she admits.

It's one thing coming up with such a brilliant idea; needless to say, the amount of work involved in the labs, developing, refining, testing and checking is enormous. The next stage is perhaps even harder – persuading the construction industry to use the material. It's not surprising that the industry can be quite conservative in adopting new technology. In a way it has to be – they need to know that the materials they use are durable, tested and safe. But Concrete4Change are making great strides and have partnered with some of the largest construction companies out there. It is helped by the fact that the construction industry knows that it has to make real changes if it is to transition to net zero over the coming years. The amazing thing is that if this were to become widely adopted, the concrete industry could go further than that and actually become net negative. And ultimately, because the concrete is stronger, the construction industry is also looking at reduced costs – up to 70 per cent – potentially making it a hugely attractive proposition.

Given how game-changing this has the power to be, I'm not surprised to hear that Concrete4Change won the United Nations most innovative net zero technology award at COP26 in 2022, and has garnered a whole host of other awards, from the SEG award to the Royal Academy of Engineering Prize.

The company is still small, but its horizons are enormous: 'The ultimate ambition would be that all concrete would be this type of concrete in the foreseeable future,' says Aisling. It is definitely punching above its weight.

This is what makes a hero of innovation, in my opinion. It's difficult to claim that concrete is a glamorous subject, or one that will easily win dramatic headlines. But this is sometimes the way real change comes – brilliant people doggedly working on ideas that might not seem flashy, but that do something radical. The climate change crisis is, quite frankly, terrifying. It's a man-made issue and one that the great machine of progress sometimes seems powerless to stop. There is no such thing as one simple solution to stop it in its tracks. Ultimately, we have to stop producing CO_2 in the amounts we do, and that is a difficult thing to achieve. But it makes me sleep a little better at night knowing that there are people out there, like the team at Concrete4Change, who are using all their ingenuity to tackle the problem as it stands. So concrete may not sound like the sexiest of materials, but what Concrete4Change have the potential to achieve... That is something pretty cool.

Fionn Ferreira

What were you doing when you were 12 years old? If you were anything like me, you might have been building spaceships with LEGO and using them to shoot your sibling's constructions out of the sky. Recently, I met someone who, when he was 12, was putting his LEGO to a much more interesting use: inventing devices to investigate environmental pollution in the sea next to where he lived. Fionn Ferreira is still incredibly young by my standards (he's only 21), but already the ideas from those early LEGO contraptions have evolved into something really extraordinary. While he was still a teenager, he came up with a way of removing microplastics from water. That is – he is looking at a solution to one of the most pressing ecological problems we have. 'I didn't have a brother,' he says with a laugh when I point out the differences between us, 'so I chose something else that annoyed me: the plastic on the shore.'

Fionn grew up in West Cork, Ireland, and as a child he was always in tune with the environment – he loved to be out and about in nature, kayaking or sailing or pottering about on the coast. But even at that age, he couldn't help but notice the huge amounts of plastic washed up on the beach. At the time – this was around nine years ago – there wasn't much of a conversation going on about the amount of plastic in our waters, but Fionn started to think that if he could see all these large pieces of plastic, there might be more that he couldn't see. When he wasn't outside in nature ('It rains a lot in Ireland') what he liked to do most was to play around with his LEGO and invent machines. He was going through a phase of constructing devices that could measure things – he would use temperature sensors, or make little weather stations. Being Fionn, he decided the next logical step was to make a machine that used visible light spectroscopy to measure the amount of plastic that was in the water. Putting it simply (which he has to for me – I'm not the most scientific of people), he would shine a light at a sample of water; any plastic in the sample would absorb some of that light, and a spectrometer would measure how the light had changed, and therefore how much plastic was present. Simple, right?

Measuring the plastics was one thing – what that did was to confirm to Fionn that there was a serious problem: the water was indeed full of microplastics. This was all pretty impressive in someone so young, but it was the next step that was so revolutionary: he began to think, 'Well, what if I try removing plastic from the water?'

★

Before telling you how he started to go about doing so, I just want to pause for a moment to think about that question he asked himself – because to be honest, that question is why Fionn is one of my humble heroes. I think he comes from a deeply impressive generation – we see it in young activists, most famously Greta Thunberg, but also all the other hundreds of thousands of young people who see problems in the world, and don't just accept them or rail against them, but take the next step and think what they can do to change things. It's as if they don't see barriers, they see challenges. In lots of cases, the tools they use are activism or protest. Fionn took a different approach and brought his natural scientific curiosity to bear. At the age of around 13, he was passionate about the environment he loved, and 'felt very angry about the problems' that were facing it. But he didn't just let the anger fester, he didn't see any reason why he shouldn't try to fix things. As he puts it, 'A lot of people think the cutting edge is very far away, a lot of people think these problems are so, so difficult to solve. But they don't realise they're actually quite close to us, we just need to narrow our field down enough that we're close to the cutting edge.'

I find this inspirational. There is no doubt that Fionn's incredibly fertile scientific mind is exceptional. But in my book he's a hero because of his attitude: if you see a problem, you don't just wait for someone else to come along and fix things – it's more interesting to see what you can do about it yourself. That attitude lies at the heart of his whole approach: if you want the plastic gone from your beloved ocean, what's stopping you from inventing a machine to remove it? It's interesting that Fionn's parents were both very practical people. They are traditional wooden boat builders, and their attitude, says Fionn, has always been that 'anything can be built'. For Fionn,

'It was always valuable to know that I could build any piece of equipment I wanted with what we had at home... If I wanted a box, they'd make me a box.' As a young teenager, he 'really just loved the process of building and being involved, and having my whole desk full of electrical components'. Not that it didn't sometimes get him into a bit of a pickle. There was the time when he was after a 'really high-power light source with a big spectral range, and I needed quite a lot of power, but I kind of short-circuited the power for my whole village...' He didn't confine himself to plastic removal either: at one point he also built a machine to 'analyse the antioxidant content of berries, because we had a lot of berry bushes'.

I have to say, at this point I am irresistibly reminded of Flint Lockwood, hero of the excellent Disney film *Cloudy with a Chance of Meatballs* – a teenager with a crazy inventing laboratory in his back garden who comes up with all kinds of extraordinary contraptions. Fionn is such a fantastic mix of enthusiasm and inquisitiveness – it's obvious he just loves the process of thinking and building and inventing, and he's incredibly invigorating company. I defy anyone to spend half an hour with him and not come away thinking it's possible to change the world.

But on a more serious level, that process of invention is not just bright ideas and lightbulb moments of inspiration: it is a painstaking process requiring large amounts of scientific knowledge, trial and error, testing and retesting, and the willingness to keep going when things don't go right. His original spectrometer didn't come about overnight, it was a gradual progression: 'It started with really simple measurements and then it got more and more developed till it turned into quite a complex machine that could do quite a lot.' He still has that original LEGO measuring device in his student accommodation.

★

To go back to that crucial question, then – having identified the problem with his measuring device, could he try removing plastics from the water? The answer he gave himself was, yes, why not? So he came up with a method that uses ferromagnetic fluids – essentially magnetic liquids – to attach themselves to the particles of plastic suspended in the water. He can then use a magnet to attract and remove the particles. It sounds completely ingenious, and Fionn found when he tested and retested and retested over 4,000 times (he had to build himself a device to keep repeating the extraction), that it did in fact work. On his website, you can see a video of the basic principle at work in a laboratory flask: it's almost magical, while of course being entirely scientific. (According to Fionn, people who enjoy watching ASMR clips on TikTok should try getting into chemistry – 'It's so much more satisfying.') How did it feel when he realised that his theoretical concept was working in practice? 'It happened quite gradually, but it's a really good feeling. I'd recommend it as something you should try.'

Proving the idea would work in practice was the first step. The next was to try and get people to take it seriously, because not surprisingly it was hard to get them to listen to a teenager from Ireland. He took the invention to Ireland's Young Scientist Competition in 2018, which he won, and from there on to various other science fairs, culminating in the 2019 Google Science Fair, at which he won the global grand prize. All of this 'gave me a platform to reach out to scientists to get funding,' Fionn says, and it has allowed him to move the invention on from a lab-based idea into the engineering phase. Through a grant from Robert Downey Jr's FootPrint Coalition, he is working with a lab in Ohio, where they are currently in prototype mode for a device which can clean plastics out of water on a household scale, 'maybe to clean water entering your house so you don't drink plastics in your drinking water.' Next on the horizon is to try and develop a prototype that will work on the scale of a river or stream, or most importantly at a point where a lot of plastics are entering the environment, such as a waste water treatment flow. The first priority, he believes, is to try and stop more plastics entering the ocean. After that we can look to clean up what is already there.

Fionn is excited by the prospect of these hopes becoming realities in the next couple of years. But he is also clear that they are not the solution: 'The solution is that we stop making plastic and releasing it into the environment in the first place. Until we solve that we are not going to win this battle.' It is not that he wants to set himself up in direct opposition to the plastics industry – as he says, plastic is a good, strong, robust material while it is in use. The problems come with the fact that we haven't come up with a good way to deal with its end life. He would like to see plastic redesigned so that it can break down naturally: 'And we can only achieve that if we work together with existing companies, so there's no point standing in the way and opposing ourselves to them.'

★

It won't surprise you to hear that there are lots of other problems Fionn would love to address – anyone as passionate and connected to the environment as he is couldn't fail to see a lot that they would like to fix. He is currently a student in the Netherlands, completing his Bachelor research programme. But he is trying to prioritise the things that he feels he can do to really make a difference: 'I don't want to waste time with things that are not going to make a difference, because I think it's important we act so soon.' Amazingly, given the enormous number of accolades he has already won – including a Forbes 30 under-30 citation – and all he has achieved when he is barely out of his teens, he still feels he is not doing enough, and he wants other people to feel the same way: 'Because I think if everybody feels they're not doing enough, then we're in a really, really good place to make a difference.'

Fionn is passionate about inspiring other people – especially other young people – to take up the challenge of invention. He believes in the power of storytelling in science, and carries out public speaking and runs workshops to do what he can to spread his message. Ultimately, he says, 'I want more youth to aspire to invent. Because I think we as youth have the power to make a difference... If what I have achieved with a couple of pieces of LEGO so far has even the slightest impact of inspiring youth to take action, imagine the things that all youth can do together.'

I came away from talking to Fionn feeling strangely reassured and optimistic, and it took me a moment to work out why. (It wasn't because of his scientific brilliance, which just made me wish I had paid a lot more attention in school.) I think it is because if there are many more people in Fionn's generation with his spark and energy and determination – and I believe there are – then there is a huge amount for the world to be hopeful about.

Katrin McMillan

E very now and then, you meet somebody you really feel
might change the planet. That is certainly how I felt
recently when I met Katrin McMillan, the founder of the charity
Hello World.

In a way, Katrin's journey to becoming a hero of innovation
started with some fairly simple arithmetic. At that time, 14
years ago, she was living in Nigeria, and as she travelled
around the country for her work with various international
aid agencies, she couldn't help but notice that in every
corner of the country you could find derelict schools – built
some years before by philanthropists who were full of good
intentions – but which had somehow not been supported or
supplied with proper resources as the years had passed and
were now abandoned. The sight of these schools set her off
thinking about education on a global scale, and as she dug
into the facts and figures, she began to realise that they really
didn't add up.

Here are the numbers that started to get her thinking, and make her, in her own words 'really quite pissed off'. One in five children round the world have no access to education at all. That is 256 million children – a terrifyingly large number – who simply aren't being educated. And even among those who do make it to school, a substantial proportion are at schools that are woefully substandard and under-resourced. Worldwide, there is an enormous deficit of teachers: even to hit the very, very low standards of education targets we set, there are 70 million too few of them.

In other words, there are millions and millions of children who have no hope of receiving an education. Katrin realised that 'even if we combined all the money out there and applied it to schools and teachers we wouldn't come close to reaching every child.' It was becoming clear to her that we just didn't have any meaningful way of solving the education deficit on a global scale.

This subject became a bit of an obsession with her, even as she moved countries and jobs and ended up in Ethiopia. She looked and looked for ways of solving it, and in the course of her research, she came across a TED Talk by a man called Sugata Mitra, who in 1999 had come up with an extraordinary experiment. In what he called the 'Hole in the Wall' experiment, he had embedded some screens, fully connected to high-speed internet, into the walls of a slum in New Delhi, and left them there for the children to use as they wanted. He was trying to understand if children could, if absolutely necessary, 'become functionally and effectively autodidactic just by using the internet', as Katrin puts it. That is, can children teach themselves, if they are given the resources to do so? The Hole in the Wall project was an extraordinary success – the results he got from that first experiment, and the subsequent ones he conducted round India and beyond, showed that groups of children, if left alone with the web, could achieve some quite extraordinary feats of learning. (If you've never watched his TED Talk, I urge you to find it: it's absolutely fascinating.)

That TED Talk unlocked something for Katrin. Suddenly, the whole problem she was wrestling became flipped on its head, because rather than come at the issue from the insoluble angle of having to magic up a global cohort of teachers out of nothing, Katrin realised it might be possible to try a completely different and radical approach.

Not surprisingly, Sugata Mitra was a hard man to get hold of at that time – it was 2013, his talk had just won the TED Prize, he was very much sought after. But, 'I called him and I called him and I called him again… and eventually he picked up the phone and said, "You're very tenacious, what do you want?"' And Katrin said, 'I need you to teach me everything you've learned.'

To go back a step, throughout the previous 20 years of working with big aid agencies in international development, Katrin had found that the things she had been most passionate about were the small-scale projects she worked on in a personal capacity. Things like helping found a women's collective that made soap, or building a house made of recycled plastic bottles. She had found that these community-led projects were very much where her heart lay: she believed deeply that progress was most effective and most deep-rooted when it sprang from within communities themselves, and when those communities were at the heart of any decision-making process.

So when she spoke to Sugata Mitra, her thinking was that she might be able to find a way of combining her on-the-ground knowledge of developing community-led projects with the insights that his experiments had given him. Sugata's premise was that children are capable of teaching themselves, if they can get access to the internet. Katrin's self-imposed challenge was to take this understanding, and think about how to provide that access in the least accessible of places. Could she come up with some way of doing this, she asked herself, that would be 'rugged enough, robust enough, adaptable for extreme conditions. That would be affordable, lasting, and that, ultimately, we could scale to reach many millions of people who currently don't go to school?' What she set out to design therefore was a way for 'remote last-mile communities, living in extreme poverty, to access unlimited, world-class educational resources, and unlimited internet.'

I mean, as an idea, that sounds absolutely and totally amazing. But it also sounds next door to impossible. And yet, it was exactly what Katrin did. She came up with the idea of the Hello Hub. I'll let Katrin describe it herself: 'A Hello Hub is an outdoor, solar-powered, internet-connected computer kiosk, with eight public, rugged touch screens that are loaded with world-class educational software and available 24 hours a day... It has free and totally unlimited high-speed internet for the entire community to use.' In other words, it is a method of bringing 21st-century technology to anywhere in the world, no matter how little infrastructure exists there.

Now, that sounds impressive at first hearing, but if you think about it, it's more than just impressive, it's revolutionary. What Katrin is talking about when she says 'last mile communities' are villages that not only have never had the internet, they have never even had power. She's talking about places where there have simply never been the resources to build, and supply schools, let alone to find teachers, and where this has meant that the lack of education is multi-generational. These are communities which have been cut off from the progress the developed world takes for granted. Her invention could give them a portal to step into the modern age.

I admit, when Katrin first told me about the hubs, I could barely imagine what this might look like. In fact, every part of the hub is incredibly cleverly designed. The hub itself comes in a purpose-built crate that is not too big so it is possible to transport. The solar panels are tiles, which allows them to fit inside, and the crate itself becomes part of the hub when dismantled. (If lack of constant sun is a problem, the hub can also be powered by a bike.) The screens are tested to the nth degree to make sure that they are waterproof, heatproof and dustproof, and they are a decent size so that they can be used by more than one person at a time (in Sugata Mitra's work, a key finding was that the self-learning was effective when it took place in a group). The whole thing is usually housed inside a specially designed geodesic dome to shelter it from the weather – something easily assembled, and whose upper panels can be decorated by the children – or sometimes the community prefers to house it in an existing structure, or use a bus-shelter style construction. It is lit all night long so it's safe for children to work through the night, and it is built in a central, public space so that it becomes part of the heart of the community.

Here are some more statistics: the first hub was built in 2013, in Suleja, Nigeria. By 2109 the team had built 33 in Uganda, eight in a refugee camp. In 2019, HelloWorld set up a team in Nepal, and has now built 14 hubs there. Typically, the hubs are in use for 19 and a half hours a day, and roughly 1,200 people use each one. All of which means that in the nine years since HelloWorld launched, it has brought connection to a truly extraordinary number of people. Sugata Mitra himself has said: 'The Hello Hub to me is like a grandchild of the Hole in the Wall, 16 years later.'

★

And how has it gone? Truthfully, it's been amazing. Hello Hubs have achieved things they could barely have hoped for, though Katrin would probably say in other ways there is still a long way to go. The possibilities that come with the hub are endless. The idea might have sprung out of Katrin's desire to improve access to education, but the uses it is put to in practice have encompassed and far surpassed that initial aim. As Katrin describes it, each hub is somewhere the community 'can participate in the internet; solve problems; unlock their potential; build businesses, make music. We have lots of farmers checking the weather to see when to sow seeds; lots of people doing health research as we all did during Covid.'

The hubs can also be the vehicle for entirely different development projects: a way for the community to access cooperative savings or loans, or vocational training. (A lot of cake-making businesses and hair-braiding enterprises have sprung up from Hello Hub users.) Katrin is particularly excited by the mentoring – and reverse mentoring – programmes that the hubs facilitate: in other words, someone on a hub can teach you Swahili while you teach them English. (Again, this harks back to Sugata Mitra's research. He set up what he called a Granny Cloud, where older generations provided gentle encouragement to his groups of learners, and it had a galvanising effect.)

As for the education side – this has been happening at every stage of life: 81 per cent of users in Uganda say they have learned a new skill; 75 per cent of people who use the hubs are of school age, and a full quarter of those have no other schooling. That is an extraordinary thing. Embedded in those figures are hundreds of children for whom the hub is their only educational tool. And they are doing amazing things with it: children using the Hello Hubs have participated in the Global Young Journalists Awards – a prestigious international competition to encourage the next generation of reporters and journalists, judged by such luminaries as Tina Fey. Nearly a third of the entries for last year's competition came from Hello Hub users, young writers who suddenly had the ability to share their stories with the world.

And all of that is not even to take into account the emotional, psychological role the hubs have played. It was in Nepal, where the Hello Hubs launched in 2019, that Katrin saw the crystallisation of one use of the hub that she hadn't even considered when she first came up with the idea. In much of rural Nepal, a lot of the parent-age generation have to leave their villages and go either to cities or abroad to the Middle East to find work, often in very difficult, bonded-labour situations. Typically, they will have to leave their children behind to be looked after by the grandparents: it is a hollowing out of the population that is desperately sad. Given that, it probably shouldn't have been a surprise when she was there for the installation of a hub, and saw that the first thing people did as it went live and they could get online was to start FaceTiming their loved ones. These were people who hadn't seen each other in months, sometimes in years. Katrin backed away to give them privacy: it was a moment that threatened to overwhelm her.

A similar thing happened as the hubs started to go into refugee camps. So many children in those camps have fled the most dire of situations, and are existing in the camps on a budget of the 20p a day that they are given by the UN. That is barely enough for clean water and food; data of any kind is clearly out of the question. But the free food and power offered by a Hello Hub (each hub offers free solar-powered energy as well) allows them to stay in touch with the loved ones they have left behind.

As I listen to Katrin tell me about all this – and trust me, I could listen to her all day, such is her passion for the project and so amazing are the things the hub has achieved – an image pops into my mind that is nothing to do with 21st-century technology, or data, or screens. It is an image of the village pump – that old, old piece of kit that for century on century has lain at the heart of village life, a place for people to gather, talk and be together, receiving the essential element that keeps their community going. Perhaps it's a bit fanciful, but it sounds to me like the hub is a new, high-tech version of that, feeding the community with a new kind of lifeblood.

★

The idea for Hello World is so radical and so potentially revolutionary that I'm curious to know how it was received when Katrin first came up with it. Back then, it wasn't an easy sell. She was 'laughed out of meeting rooms' with the recurring opinion being that children can't learn on the internet: 'All they're going to do is watch Beyoncé videos,' was a typical response.

To which I completely agree with Katrin's riposte: 'I think it's OK to watch Beyoncé videos. Maybe they're watching it for fun. Fun is good. Or maybe they're watching it to learn the dance. Dance is good.'

But the overall message she was hearing boiled down to the notion that the internet was a luxury – something that might be nice to have, but which was essentially extraneous in the kind of places she was talking about. Oddly, in spite of the fact that in 2016 the UN declared access to the internet to be a human right, it was actually the global pandemic that began finally to bring about a change in this attitude. Suddenly everyone in the world could not just see but actually feel exactly what access to the internet means. That it is the difference between total isolation and being able to talk to your loved ones. That it can provide a space for children, however reluctantly, to carry on with their lessons when suddenly a classroom and a teacher are not available. That it is a vehicle for both adults and children 'to learn and play and express themselves'. The idea that the internet is nothing but a frivolous add-on to life suddenly became untenable.

Nevertheless, it remains true that what we call the World Wide Web is anything but. I started out by giving you some figures that Katrin shared with me – here is another one:

40 per cent of the world still has no access to the internet. Forty per cent! This is the medium we consider to be the repository of the world's knowledge and yet, as Katrin puts it, this enormous slice of humanity 'is still on mute'. She adds: 'We're not hearing from them; we're not hearing their ideas, we're not hearing about their land, we're not capturing their language.' You would think that there would be a scramble to provide connection, and yet, says Katrin, 'I am in competition with nobody to reach those people.'

There is still such a hugely long way to go. Which is why what Katrin really wants to happen next is for others to take on the approach and run with it. To this end, just like the guys at Team UnLimbited, Hello World have ensured that the plans for the hubs are open source. On the website you can find an entire section that is a how-to guide to building a hub. Everything is on there, in as accessible a form as possible: shopping lists of what is needed, videos on how to build the shelter, instructional manuals... all at your fingertips. If you wanted to build a Hello Hub, they have made it as easy as possible. 'My organisation is tiny and our capacity is limited, and the best way to get to scale is to amplify our work so that other people can apply their cultural knowledge, their imagination and their energy,' Katrin says. She envisions a world where others take what she has created and run with it, reaching as many people around the world as possible.

★

I try to imagine what it feels like for these communities when a Hello Hub first arrives: it must be as though something from out of space has landed in their village. And on one level it is.

But what is also revolutionary is that this is not just a question of taking a pre-formed pod and placing it in a community and seeing what happens: the community builds the hub itself. Down to her bones, Katrin is convinced that what is most important in any international development project is that the communities that are being helped must be at the forefront of decision making. She wanted Hello World to get as far away as possible from the mindset that we 'identify problems from Silicon Valley or Paris or London or New York, come up with a solution, foist it on an unsuspecting community, expect them to be incredibly grateful, get some non-consensual photos and get out again.' She wanted any community that was taking on a Hello Hub to be at the heart of the process.

What this looks like in practice is entering into discussions with the community right from the outset. It won't surprise you to hear that taking a Hello Hub and installing it in a community that has never had such a thing before comes with quite a few challenges. In fact, says Katrin, 'Until you are having a difficult, robust conversation with a community about who it's for, who has access, how do we protect it, then you haven't really begun.' The hubs are as cost-effective as possible, but we are still talking about thousands of pounds worth of technology – I love the way Katrin mentions almost as an aside that the technology in the hubs was designed pro-bono by NASA – in a community which is by definition at the very hard edge of poverty. We are also talking about communities that have their own internal hierarchies, as likely as not pretty patriarchal in nature. In refugee camps, to make things even more complicated, the hubs are going into highly complex and sometimes febrile societies that comprise many different nationalities and their corresponding divisions. All of these people are going to have to share one hub. What is going to ensure that access to the hub is equal and fair?

The answer, says Katrin, is that it is up to the community to decide. That is not to say that she doesn't make sure the conversation happens: her team's job is to facilitate these discussions and make sure everything is thrashed out in the weeks leading up to the hub being built. She will often find herself on the receiving end of comments from the community along the lines of 'This sounds expensive: this is going to get stolen.'

To which she will say, 'Oh dear, that is not good. I'm very sorry to hear that.'

This is where, she finds, the conversation really starts – 'But we can't let it get stolen.'

'No, of course. That would be terrible. What do you think the solution should be?'

What she finds interesting is that as these conversations are played out, nine times out of ten the conclusion becomes that if everybody in the community has use of the hub, then everybody has a stake and the whole community becomes responsible. It helps that the hubs are usually placed in a central location and that the usage is so high – if they are constantly buzzing with life, the chances of vandalism are slim.

The fact that the hubs are built by the community is also a key factor: a pre-fabricated block might well be easier and cheaper to install, but by asking the community to put the hub together, from the building to the engineering work, not only does the hub get rooted more organically into the community, but they are also embedding the skills to maintain and repair it. The team likes to employ a community support officer for the hub who comes from within the community, whose job is to keep the hub in order, help people to use it, show people the resources embedded in the programmes, and keep the whole thing ticking over.

This whole approach does take longer: 'It takes more patience, it takes a greater tolerance to failure, and it takes being able to pivot and change.' But Katrin can't imagine doing it any other way: the way she sees it, it is the only way to make the enterprise lasting.

★

One further issue that Hello World has had to consider is the nature of the internet itself. Those of us who use the internet day in, day out know, often to our cost, that it is not always an entirely reliable tool. Much as it has the capacity to connect and educate and enrich, we all know that it can be a scary, sometimes crazy and oddly dangerous place. There are people on there who are not who they pretend to be, and information on there that is not all it seems. Not to mention the porn... (It has always amused Katrin that when she started to pitch the idea, the question of porn always springs up from the men in the room.) Again, the team is upfront in conversations about this before the hubs go in. Robust conversations have to take place, conversations that can be difficult because they run up against some pretty fundamental structures such as religion, ethnicity, gender and age.

Balancing this out, Katrin has found that providing a relatively neutral resource has allowed families to investigate and explore things like female genital mutilation, and come away from that research with a different viewpoint. It can allow people to get away from the 'bubble of influence' of their immediate community and form their own views, and those difficult conversations can be the genesis of a new discussion within the community and allow in different ways of thinking.

One of the most exciting new ventures bubbling away in Katrin's brain is something that she hopes will counter the effects of the misinformation that the internet can bring. The Newspaper in a Box scheme will take advantage of the facilities that the Hello Hub provides and allow the communities to produce their own newspapers, professionally moderated but community written and dedicated to local news. The very experienced newspaper editor Richard Addis will be going out to Uganda in 2022 to meet the winners of the Global Journalism awards, and to advise on how to launch the new scheme. I can't wait to hear how it goes.

As for porn, the team can and do put parental controls on the screens if the community asks them to, though as we all know, there is no such thing as a parental control that can't be hacked if someone is really determined. Again, the remedy is conversation – and the fact that the hubs are typically extremely busy and in a very public space. ('It's really unlikely you're going to watch porn if your granny could walk past at any moment,' says Katrin.) In fact, analysis of the searches on the hubs shows that searches for porn are remarkably low.

★

The Hello World story is such a fantastic one, and the people who make it happen are clearly such a family – from the people on the ground in Uganda and Nepal to all the different people who make it happen worldwide, that I think the entire team deserve to be called humble heroes. But on top of that I would give a special shout-out to Katrin herself, in whose amazingly optimistic brain this all came together. She is absolutely a whirlwind of determination, and I can only imagine what skills of persuasion and force she had to use to bring all this about. Did I mention also that she has four children? In fact she was pregnant with the eldest when the first hub was launched, and has unapologetically had to hold meetings with babies in tow all along the way. When the team launched in Nepal, she brought the children with her, and they played with the village children – communicating despite the lack of a common language – while she spoke to their parents. It was an approach that underlined to her both the importance of the work she was doing, and the reasons why she personally felt the need to keep going: 'It humanised me with the mothers I work with, because we all have that common concern, that our children be safe, that they be healthy, that they have opportunities.' And on top of that, she wants her children eventually to know that she at least had a go at trying to make the world a fairer place: 'because it's not fair for anybody until it's fair for everybody.'

Hello World is doing so much to try and achieve that fairness of opportunity. It has only been going for nine years, but already there are so many stories encapsulating how extraordinary its impact has been. One of Katrin's favourites springs from one of the very first hubs built in Uganda. One day as the hub was being built a young boy called Tabu turned up. He hadn't come because of the hub – he came from nearby and had heard that there was a particularly beautiful girl in the village. After he had walked the two hours to get there, he discovered this great hubbub going on: solar panels being unloaded, people building, all sorts of activity. He hung around, and came back the next day and the next to join in. Within months, this young boy, an orphan, was a member of the Hello World team. Nowadays, self-taught on the Hello World hub, he is a successful filmmaker and photographer, and has become an activist himself. He has now been elected as President of Youth Action Uganda, and has been chosen by Sarah Brown as one of her youth ambassadors. 'I can no longer afford to hire him!' says Katrin. Or there is Sepi, who was employed by the team as Community Support Officer at the Kabahinda hub in Nakivale Refugee Settlement, Uganda, and who is now moving to Kampala, armed with the skills he has honed at the hub, to study automotive mechanics.

The Hello World website is full of wonderful stories like this, and full also of statistics that give a snapshot not only of the fantastic impact it is having, but the sheer hard work that must have gone in to achieving what it has. But however impressive those figures are, I don't think dry statistics can really get across the sheer out-of-this-world magic of what Katrin and her team are beginning to achieve. Instead, I'm going to share a story that Katrin told me, about a moment she had when installing a hub in Northern Nigeria.

She was working with a group of local teachers, trying to explain to them what the internet was, and, as she freely admits, making an appalling mess of it: 'In the sky there's a satellite, and a satellite is like an enormous bumble bee made of metal, and....' Giving up in despair, she told them she would come back the next day, and this time she would bring a dongle and her computer. In the meantime, could they think of some questions they'd like to explore online? So the next day she did just that, and together they went on a voyage of discovery: they looked at maps and satellite images of Nigeria on Google Earth; they watched videos of penguins skidding about on icefloes and dolphins leaping out of the water; they asked lots of questions about health issues and got the answers; they laughed at funny clips and listened to music. Basically, they did the kind of things we all do online all the time. And then one woman, a teacher, put her hand up.

'This internet, does he know any lesson plans?'

'Well,' said Katrin, 'what are you teaching the children about at the moment?'

The answer was that they were learning about the taste buds. So together, the group looked up taste buds online, and of course there were reams and reams of pages all about them. What happened next took Katrin by surprise: 'The woman started to cry and the group closed around her, and I wasn't sure what was going on. And when she came up for breath, she explained to me: "For 15 years I have been trying to help the children in my community have a better life. And I have been trying to do that with no books, nothing to give them the education they need. And I didn't know that everything I needed to teach them, it was in the air."'

At that moment, it must have been as though everything came full circle for Katrin. Hello World had started with her desire to provide an access to education to children who simply never were going to be able to sit in a school with a teacher and a classroom. But in that moment she saw that it was not just for the children – it was for the teachers, and the parents, and the grandmothers and the babies. It was for everyone who wasn't being given the resources or the ability to have a voice in this world.

What had started out being a tool for educating children could be so much more. 'The truth is, it's for the community to decide what they do with this resource,' says Katrin now. 'And they never fail to amaze me.'

I think amazing is pretty much the word.

Afterword

My goodness: how to sum up the incredible experience that I have had writing this book? Right at the beginning, when I came up with this humble heroes idea, it was because everything seemed to be so bleak. We were in the heart of the first of the lockdowns, the news agenda was full of negativity and conflict, and wherever you looked there seemed to be some story about how everything was getting worse. And let's be honest, there is no doubt that there is plenty to be worried about in the world. But I was convinced that underneath all this bleakness there were a whole load of other stories we weren't getting to hear. I had a feeling that the news we were hearing masked a different and valuable truth: that brilliant things are being done by brilliant people, that though there are many problems we are never far away from someone that is trying to help, and that, together, all these efforts add up to something great.

That thought turned first of all into a series of Instagram

interviews, and a callout on social media, and finally into this book. And through it all, at every stage, my conviction has been proved right: there seems to be no shortage of people who want to make the world better. I've come away from each encounter feeling humbled myself – sometimes with my mind blown by the brilliance and ingenuity of the people that I've met, sometimes with my heart broken at what they have had to face, often just in awe of the sheer energy and passion they put into their causes. The heroes I have met come from such varied walks of life, from different age groups and different communities, with projects on scales that range from the specific and local to the world-changing. Every single one of them has given me something new to think about. Every single one of them has made me grateful, and optimistic. It's been a pleasure and an honour to get to know them and hear their stories.

★

So apart from making me (and you too, I hope) feel a whole lot better, are there any broader lessons that I can take from my fantastic group of humble heroes? Almost too many to list, perhaps.

Gabby Edlin, one of the heroes that I met (and we know she won't thank me for that title), said something that really stayed with me. She told me that she and her team tried to go about her work with joy, and with anger – 'the two most useful emotions,' as she put it. Funnily enough, the day after I spoke to Gabby, I was talking to Fionn Ferreira, an encounter that left me just brimming with optimism for the next generation. And in what he said I heard an echo of her words – he described how as a young boy he was filled with anger at the desecration of the environment he loved. But he didn't let the emotion envelop him: he used it as a spur, and set about finding solutions in the most joyful way he knew – through science. What he wants most of all now – besides the removal of all the plastic from the seas – is to inspire other people to feel those things along with him. As he sees it, if enough people want to change things, and use every tool at their disposal to do so, then the world is closer to change than we think.

As I thought about this, I realised that those two emotions – joy and anger – gleam through so many of the stories I have heard while writing this book. The anger is what moves you to want to change things; the joy is what makes it work. There is joy flowing through the pages of this book: it's how Carrie described the feeling in her yard. It's in the moments that the Team UnLimbited kids unwrap their parcels; it's in the smiles when a long-lost face is beamed across the internet by a Hello Hub.

It is the joy that I find especially interesting, because it seems to me that all these people are not only bringing joy to their causes, but are gaining exponential amounts of it back in return. I heard variations of the same thing again and again, from people who had done amazing things for others, had worked late into the night or put their bodies through superhuman feats: 'You get back more than you put in.' So many of the heroes were just overflowing with the energy of a job worth doing, from Shelley Hart putting her all into building up a fantastic volunteer centre, to Aaron Hill bringing football to those 140 girls in his club. When you think of how much these people achieve – often on the back of a full-time job or a demanding family – you can only assume that this joy is in itself a superpower. How else do they get so much done?

There's no doubt there were times when what all these people were doing made me feel very inadequate – thinking about what young Heather or Ryan have achieved before they are out of their teens, or what Josh, Vicky and Ivan put themselves through, or the way Damien and his crew are willing to risk their lives to save others, is enough to make you feel a little small. I have sometimes left my encounters with these heroes wondering what on earth I have been doing with my time. But this feeling has been pretty short-lived, because again and again what I heard from all the people I've spoken to is that anybody can have a go at doing something good. That first step can feel like the hardest barrier, but that's only in our minds. As Fionn says, we tend to think that all these problems are huge and the solutions are impossible, but you only find out if you can fix them when you try. So give it a go, as Ryan says, 'You'll probably like it.'

Interestingly, one thing that has made it so much easier to 'give it a go' has been social media. There can be so much discord and toxicity online that it's easy to think of it as something negative, but I've learned it can also be a fantastic force for good. Think of Kwajo, turning his Twitter feed into a one-man crusade that is changing lives all over the country. Think of Jem or Gabby, reaching out to ask for bikes or period supplies for those in need, or of Heather, whose whole family can use the internet to spread her particular brand of sunshine worldwide, all from her front room up in Scotland. Think in particular of wonderful Harry, in the months before he died, being able to reach out and touch so many people through the power of his story. The distance between impulse and execution is so much shorter now, and we have the internet to thank for that.

And that is important, because I've learned that what so many of our heroes want most of all is for others to join them. They want to be part of a worldwide conversation that makes things better, not to sit alone at the peak of the mountain marvelling at how far they've come. It's why Team UnLimbited and Hello World have made their fantastic innovations available to anyone at the click of a mouse; it's why Carrie dreams of rolling out the Stable Lives method across the country; its why Candoco takes care to make a real connection with their audiences wherever they go. Being a real humble hero isn't all about stepping into the spotlight, it's about inviting others up to share the stage.

★

There are certain images that keep coming back into my mind from all the stories I have heard. One is the thought of Kwajo's neighbour on his estate, who went for 27 years without having her kitchen fixed. That is 27 years of being ignored, 27 years of being made to feel that her problems were insignificant. Think how hopeless that must have made her feel, and then think what it was that Kwajo brought her: he brought her hope. It is hope that Redemption Roasters bring to the graduates of their courses; hope that Carrie and her wonderful horses are bringing to people who have been through trauma. The same hope that Ivan had in the forefront of his mind as he ran half the length of the country. Hope is a golden thread that weaves through every one of these stories. It's such a vital emotion, something we need in the toughest of times. But that hope is often hard-fought, hard-won. Because let's not forget that lots of these stories are stories about battles. Writing this book has been an inspirational experience, but it has also brought me face to face with the harder edges of life. So many of these people are heroes because they are standing up to change things that are wrong – whether that's the global education deficit or the fact that climate change needs to be addressed, or that LGBTQ+ people are being treated badly. We need these heroes because the world is not perfect. Sometimes you have to force the door down – and sometimes that door is swollen and stuck because an unrepaired leak has been dripping onto it for months. Sometimes you have to demand people hear you, you have to send email after email after email, or insist that things should be done differently. Hope is an enormous motivating force, and a gift you can give, but it's not always just sunbeams and smiles.

Some of these battles have been fought over years, some are crusades that are just getting going. If, as Fionn says, it sometimes seems as though the problems we are looking at are too big to contemplate, it's worth remembering how much things have changed in the last few years. Look at the difference between the world Candoco operates in now and the landscape they were born into, or how radically the armed forces have changed since the day that Craig first walked into that naval training college. Look how quickly the conversation around mental health has changed since Hussain conquered that stage a few short years ago. Things are shifting all the time, and if they are shifting for the better, it's because of heroes just like the people I have met.

★

So – joy, anger, hope and change. What else have I learned from all these fantastic people? I think the final lesson is about connection, because in the end that is a light that shines through every one of these stories. It might be the local connections that are forged through lifeboat stations or community orchards, or volunteer centres, or a drop-in centres where old and young can come together. It could be in the way a new bike can help a refugee, longing for home, connect with the new place he finds himself in. It might be the words wrung from the mind of a poet that resonate in the hearts of his audience, or the healing that a yard full of horses and welcome can bring to a traumatised veteran. It might be the connection that a group of friends, running for the best of causes, feel as they surge across a finish line. It might be in the wonder with which a child in a faraway place connects to a mentor on a Hello Hub for the first time, or in the job an inmate joins on his release. It might be in the way that Harry, using social media to raise awareness, found online a community of people who cared, who did so much to buoy him up in the worst of his illness. Or how Josh's CF warriors, unable to meet each other by the very nature of their condition, have found a community online that connects them all.

I think in the end that is what this book is about. If the last years have taught us anything, it is that connection between human beings is fundamental to who we are. It's in our very nature. We need to know that there are people out there who have our backs, who will listen to us, fight for us, or just talk to us. The heroes in these pages are people who are bringing that sense of connection to the world in all sorts of different ways. And if reading about them can inspire you to do even the smallest thing to offer hope or help or connection, then it will have been a success.

As for me, now more than ever I am primed to see heroes wherever I go – so much good in the world, so many great deeds being done. In that way, writing this book has changed my life. I hope, in some small way, it has done the same for you.

Acknowledgements

Firstly to Rebekka: your creative ideas, support, advice and guidance have turned the simplest idea into something so much bigger. Thank you isn't enough.

To Lizzie, Joe and all the team at YMU: you know I'd be lost without you – I would literally never get anywhere or do anything – so thank you for never giving up on me.

To Amanda and Anna on the books side, and to Susannah, Sophie and all the team at Bonnier: thank you so much for believing in this idea and helping to create something so special. I can't wait to see where it ends up!

To all the contributors: your passion, drive, vision and humour is what inspires me. It's been a privilege to curate this book and offer you all a platform to share your incredible work.

Crucially, to Celia – the way you have helped shape these wonderful peoples' stories, and to share not only their voices but also mine, still astonishes me. It's been such a thrill to go on this journey with you: I hope you've enjoyed it as much as me. Here's to many more!

Finally, to the heroes in my own life – Annie, Sam and Jack. They put up with more than they should, they cost me more than they should, and I wouldn't have it any other way. They are my biggest inspiration.